# THE CHESAPEAKE BAY
# FISH & FOWL COOKBOOK

# THE
# FISH &

# CHESAPEAKE BAY FOWL COOKBOOK

*A Collection of*

*Old and New Recipes*

*from Maryland's*

*Eastern Shore*

## By JOAN and JOE FOLEY

*MACMILLAN PUBLISHING CO., INC.*

*NEW YORK*

Macmillan Publishing Co., Inc.
866 Third Avenue, New York, N.Y. 10022
Collier Macmillan Canada, Ltd.

Library of Congress Cataloging in Publication Data
Main entry under title:
The Chesapeake Bay fish & fowl cookbook.
 Includes index.
 1. Cookery (Seafood) 2. Cookery, American—
Maryland. 3. Fisheries—Chesapeake Bay.
I. Foley, Joan. II. Foley, Joseph. III. Title:
Chesapeake Bay fish and fowl cookbook.
TX747.C464      641.6'9      81-2594
ISBN 0-02-539560-2      AACR2

*Illustrations by Richard Sommers*

*Designed by Philip Grushkin*

10 9 8 7 6 5 4 3 2

Printed in the United States of America

*This book is dedicated with love
to our mothers,
Kathryn and Mary.*

# CONTENTS

## ACKNOWLEDGMENTS

We'd like to thank the wonderful people of the Eastern Shore, our good friends and neighbors who for twenty years have said, "I share what I have with you,"—including the recipes in this book.

# WELCOME TO
# PLEASANT LIVING:

MADISON Vol. Fire Co.
# Country DINNER
## Baked Chicken, Oyster Fritters, Fish Cakes

*Cole Slaw, Hot Biscuits, Gravy and Trimmings,*
Plus All You Can Eat.

**Adults $1.50     Children 75¢**

*Dessert, Cake, Pie, etc. to order*

# Saturday, Nov. 7th

**Dinners Also Fixed to Take Out**

# THE LAND OF
# THE EASTERN SHORE
# OF MARYLAND

IF CAPTAIN JOHN SMITH (of the Pocahontas legend) were to sail into Chesapeake Bay country today, the residents of the Eastern Shore would be able to tell him that he knew what he was talking about even back in 1607. Adventurer-explorer Captain Smith, looking for a place where English colonists might settle, had described the area in a report to His Majesty King James of England with these words:

> Heaven and Earthe never agreed better to frame a place for man's habitation. . . .

The nine counties of the Eastern Shore in the 1980s still reflect their English heritage in towns named Oxford, Royal Oak, Cambridge, St. Michaels, Princess Anne, Easton, and Wye Mills. The first settlers also came from Ireland, Holland, France, and Spain, seeking religious freedom in this new land. A sense of history is everywhere. Here in this "Land of Pleasant Living," whose heartbeat is the magnificent Chesapeake Bay, the best of colonial days blends comfortably with the present. It is this vivid contrast of old and new, side by side, that gives the Eastern Shore its unique charm.

When it comes to the Maryland kitchen and traditional cooking, the Eastern Shore has a unique style, too. And what a style it is!

The Chesapeake Bay provides some of the finest seafood in the world. The rich soil of the Eastern Shore produces an abundance and variety of fruits and vegetables, including the famous Maryland tomato that has been acclaimed by gourmets for its distinctive flavor (lightly touched with a taste of salt).

Eastern Shore chickens have become an institution, and Roasted

Maryland Tom Turkeys are a staple not only on Thanksgiving menus but all year round in the best restaurants and on home tables.

With this as a basic larder, brimming with foods either home-grown or caught fresh from the Bay, it's no wonder that for centuries Eastern Shore cooks have been able to concoct a variety of superb dishes. Again, the mixture of the old and the new pervades the cooking of the region, and we've tried to bring that flavor to the recipes in this book.

The ideal introduction to Eastern Shore cooking, and an incredible bargain, is one of the many firehouse or church suppers that are held throughout the year. These are feasts like no other—all you can eat—with *groaning* family-style platters of oysters, ham, fried chicken, crab cakes, salads, assorted vegetables, homemade rolls, pies, cakes. The food is always fresh, and expertly prepared, and only one rule applies: bring a good appetite!

We attended our first firehouse supper twenty years ago, and not much has changed to this day including the prices. The poster modestly advertised that long ago firehouse supper, and we soon learned what "Trimmings" "Plus All You Can Eat" mean on the Eastern Shore!

Please Note: Unless otherwise stated, all recipes are intended to serve four people.

# THE CHESAPEAKE BAY
# FISH & FOWL COOKBOOK

# THE WATERS

# CHESAPEAKE BAY: CRABS

THE STARS are still out and the steady high-pitched zizz-zz of the locusts in their trees is the only sound that breaks the quiet of early morning. It is 3 A.M. and the workboats with their red and green running lights sputter as they nose into the Bay. The watermen are going to work. If all goes well within the next few hours, the trotline —a long length of rope with pieces of bait attached at three-to-four-foot intervals—will pull in many bushels of savory, beautiful swimmers, their brilliant blue claws clicking and snapping.

The "catch" is the hard-shell blue crab (or, by its scientific name, the *sapidus*—savory, *calli*—beautiful, *nectes*—swimmer) and from April to December the Chesapeake Bay yields more of this seafood delicacy than any other body of water in the world. A good day of crabbing can mean a "Crab Feast"; not that anyone in Maryland needs a special occasion to steam up a bushel of crabs. The ingredients start with congenial and hungry people who like to eat with their fingers, and then it's on to the Feast!

## HARD-SHELL CRABS

For a feast for four you'll need:

**3 cups white vinegar**

**3 cups flat beer (or water may be used)**

**½ cup salt**

**1 cup of Old Bay seasoning or other seafood seasoning**

**3 dozen live and lively hard-shell blue crabs**

Allow 6 crabs, plus 3 more in the pot, for each person. It's likely that everyone will come back for "seconds" after only 6 crabs have been picked, but you can let any leftover crabs cool at room temperature and refrigerate them within 3 hours after steaming. Crabs will keep for 3–5 days under constant refrigeration.

Everyone in Maryland has a steamer, but a large kettle or pot with a rack and a tight-fitting lid can be used instead. Pour the vinegar and beer (or water) into the pot and bring to a boil. Amateurs wear heavy gloves—the livelier crabs, especially the females, or *sooks*, can give you a nasty pinch if you don't know how to handle them. Have the lid ready to clamp on the pot as soon as you put in the crabs.

Thoroughly mix salt with Old Bay or another seafood seasoning. Add the crabs quickly, a few at a time depending on the size of your pot, and sprinkle each layer of crabs with the mixture of salt and seasoning. The seasoning gives the peppery flavor that's transferred from the crab shell to your fingers, and then to the crabmeat as you pick it from the shell and claws. More seasoning means spicier crabs, so test and taste with each steaming until you find the amount that's right for you. When all the crabs have been added, place the lid *tightly* on the pot and hold it for 1–2 minutes. You'll learn why! Steam the crabs for 25–30 minutes until they turn bright red. Remove the crabs from heat and let them cool in the pot for 2–3 minutes.

A "Crab Feast" is an informal and fun time, and the more informal the better. The crabs are turned out on a table that can be covered with newspapers, brown paper, waxed paper, or—if you insist on being fancy—a plastic tablecloth; and then it's time for everyone to dig in!

Fingers first, a knife, and a small wooden mallet (optional) will get you started. The handle of the knife, or the mallet, is used for cracking the crab claws.

All you need to serve on the side are small bowls of vinegar for dunking the crabmeat; a pepper mill for freshly ground black pepper; a big plate of saltine crackers; and plenty of over-sized paper napkins. In hot weather, there should be pitchers of ice-cold beer and ginger ale.

If you're picking your first crab at one of the feasts, it's helpful to sit next to people who know what they're doing—especially those nimble-fingered ladies who can pick a crab clean in a few seconds! We've waddled away from more empty crab shells than we could count, thanks to kindly friends and neighbors who took pity on our first bungling attempts to keep from going hungry at a feast.

Once you get the knack of it, you'll wonder why you had such difficulty picking that first crab. This is how it's done:

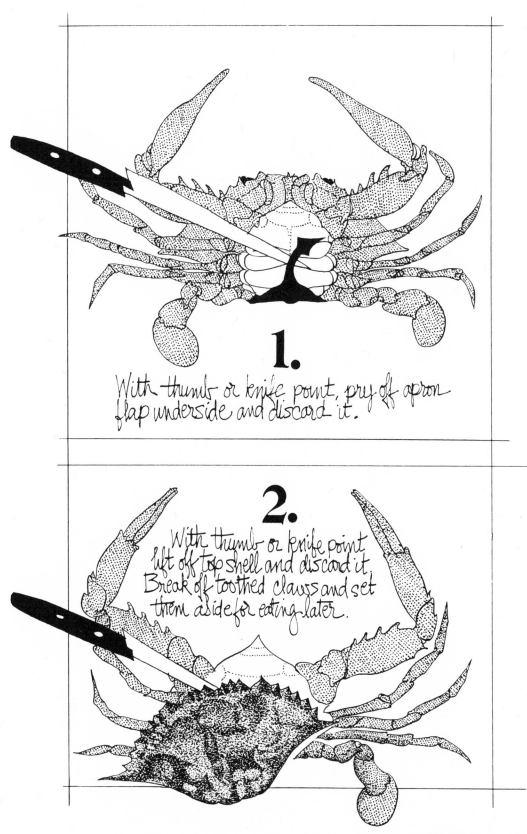

# 1.

With thumb or knife point, pry off apron flap underside and discard it.

# 2.

With thumb or knife point lift off top shell and discard it. Break off toothed claws and set them aside for eating later.

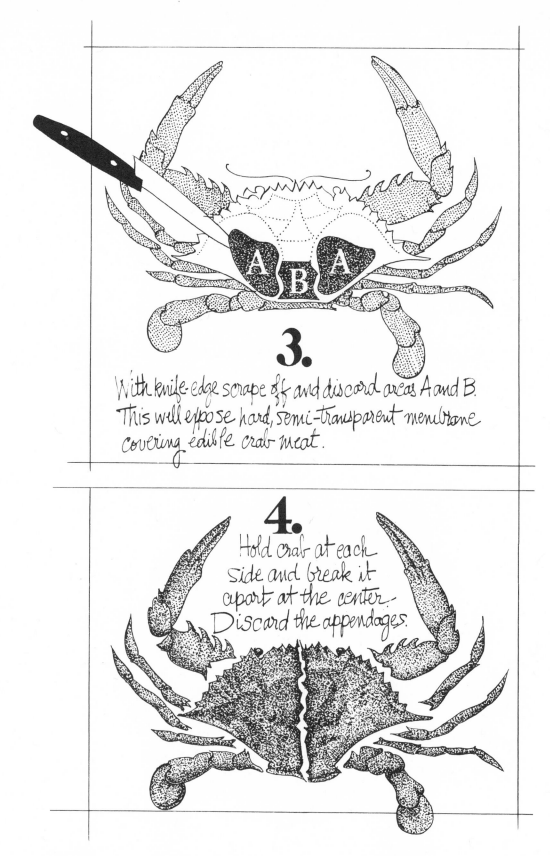

# 3.

With knife-edge scrape off and discard areas A and B. This will expose hard, semi-transparent membrane covering edible crab meat.

# 4.

Hold crab at each side and break it apart at the center. Discard the appendages.

# 5.

Meat under membrane cover in each half of crab can be exposed by removing this cover with a knife or by slicing lengthwise through the center of each half without removing the membrane. Each method will expose large, succulent chunks of meat which may be removed with a knife or fingers. Crack large claws with mallet or knife handle to expose meat within.

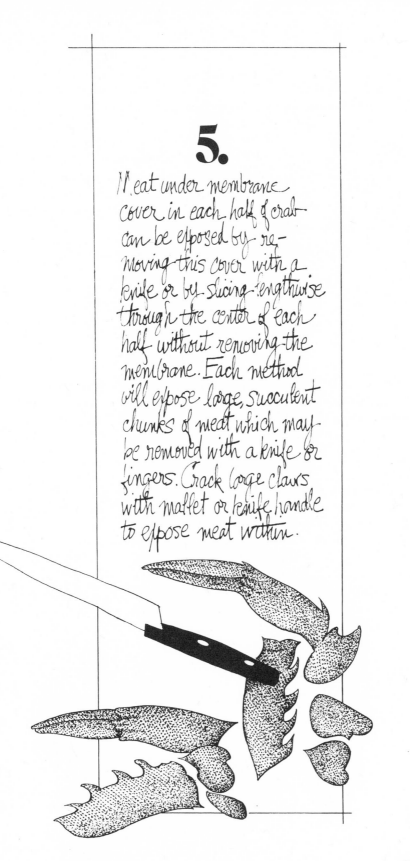

A friend in New York once asked us to bring him a dozen hard-shell crabs from Maryland, assuring us that he knew all about the steaming and picking of blue claws. He must have had some other seafood in mind because a few days later he confessed that he had attacked his dinner with a hammer, screwdriver, assorted knives, and a pair of pliers before he was able to get the meat out of the crabs. We didn't dare ask him how he had managed to *steam* them!

All recipes that follow begin with steamed crabmeat picked from the shell. A steamed crab in the shell will yield 2–3 ounces of picked crabmeat, and all cartilage should be carefully removed from the crabmeat. Crabmeat is classified as:

*Backfin*—choice whole and broken pieces of white meat
*Lump*—select larger whole pieces of backfin
*Regular*—bits and pieces of body meat
*Claw*—brownish-tinted meat from the claw
*Crab Fingers*—large biter claws of the crab with the shell partially
   removed (leaving a lump of claw meat)

Crab cakes are such a Maryland institution that we've included both plain and spicy recipes so you can decide which side to take in the ongoing debate. On one side the purists insist that high-powered spices ruin the delicate flavor of the crabmeat, while the other side argues that spices enhance it.

You'll have to taste for yourself!

Maryland pays homage often and elaborately to its crabs. The ultimate, and more unusual celebration of the blue claw crab takes place every year in Crisfield, Maryland, when the wily crustaceans are taken from the Bay; culled to get the liveliest and meanest; and entered on a dry track in the National Hard Crab Derby. This event attracts attention and visitors from all fifty states. The race is great fun, and the crabs are groomed as carefully and cheered on as enthusiastically as any Kentucky Derby entrant. A fair held at the same time as the Derby includes a crab-cooking contest; a crab-picking contest; the Crabbers' Ball; the crowning of Miss Crustacean; parades; and an endless round of activities all involving the pride of the Chesapeake. This is an exciting weekend in September that's not to be missed on the Eastern Shore.

# THE RECIPES:

CRISFIELD CRABMEAT SALAD
TIDEWATER INN CRAB IMPERIAL
BAKED CRAB FONDUE
SNOW WHITE CRAB MOUSSE
MISS LAVERNE'S CRAB IMPERIAL
JAN'S SNACKING CRABMEAT SPREAD
MRS. SMEDLEY-MOORE'S CRABMEAT SUPPER
ROSY CREAMED CRABMEAT
CREAM CRAB CAKES
HILDA'S MADISON CRAB CAKES
CRABBY BURGERS
OXFORD CRAB CAKES
SAUTÉD SOFT-SHELL CRABS
DEEP-FRIED SOFT-SHELL CRABS

## Crisfield Crabmeat Salad

½ cup mayonnaise (see recipe, page 99)

½ teaspoon salt

Sprinkling of freshly ground black pepper

1 tablespoon white vinegar

2 green onions (scallions) with tops, thinly sliced

1 small stalk celery, thinly sliced

1 small cucumber, peeled, seeded, and diced

1 small pimiento, finely chopped

1 hard-cooked egg, finely chopped

1 pound lump crabmeat

1 small head lettuce, coarsely chopped

Paprika

1 tablespoon fresh parsley, minced

Thoroughly blend mayonnaise, salt, pepper, and vinegar in a large bowl.

Add green onions, celery, cucumber, pimiento, egg, and crabmeat.

Toss lightly but well.

Cover tightly and refrigerate crab mixture for 1 hour.

Make a bed of torn or chopped lettuce on an attractive serving plate.

Toss crabmeat lightly before turning onto lettuce.

Sprinkle with paprika and parsley and serve.

Note: Extra mayonnaise may be served on the side.


## Tidewater Inn Crab Imperial

¼ cup mayonnaise (see recipe, page 99)

¾ teaspoon Worcestershire sauce

¼ teaspoon salt

Dash of Tobasco sauce

Pinch each of thyme, oregano, dry mustard

1 egg, well beaten

1 pound backfin crabmeat

1 tablespoon mayonnaise, separated

2–3 sprigs fresh parsley, minced

Paprika

Preheat oven to 350°.

Mix mayonnaise, Worcestershire, salt, Tabasco, thyme, oregano, and dry mustard in a medium-size bowl.

Stir in egg.

Gently mix in crabmeat and blend lightly but well.

Coat an attractive 1-quart casserole dish with ½ tablespoon of mayonnaise, and fill with crab mixture.

Spread remaining ½ tablespoon of mayonnaise over top of crabmeat.

Sprinkle casserole with parsley and paprika.

Bake for 35–40 minutes until piping hot and nicely browned.

## Baked Crab Fondue

4 slices white bread

2 tablespoons (¼ stick) butter, softened

1 pound lump crabmeat

1 small pimiento, finely chopped

1 cup sharp Cheddar cheese, grated, separated

2 eggs

¼ teaspoon dry mustard

½ teaspoon salt

1⅓ cup half-and-half

Paprika

¼ cup pimiento-stuffed olives, coarsely chopped (optional)

Preheat oven to 350°.

Butter bread on both sides and cut in cubes.

Line the bottom of an 8x8″ (or 8″-square) buttered baking pan with half the bread cubes.

Cover bread cubes with crabmeat, pimiento, and ½ cup of cheese.

Top crabmeat with remaining bread cubes and ½ cup of cheese.

Whisk eggs with mustard, salt, and half-and-half in a small bowl until thoroughly blended.

Pour egg mixture over all.

Sprinkle with paprika, and bake for 45 minutes until firm.

Sprinkle chopped olives (optional) over crabmeat before serving.

## Snow White Crab Mousse

*(6 servings)*

| | |
|---|---|
| **1 tablespoon unflavored gelatin** | **1 teaspoon salt** |
| **¼ cup cold water** | **Dash of paprika** |
| **¼ cup fresh lime juice** | **1 teaspoon Old Bay seasoning or other seafood seasoning** |
| **¼ cup mayonnaise (see recipe, page 99)** | **¾ cup heavy cream** |
| **1 small stalk celery, minced** | **1 tablespoon sweet (unsalted) butter** |
| **1 small cucumber, peeled, seeded, and finely diced** | **Bunch of watercress** |
| **1 pound lump crabmeat** | **¼ cup pitted green olives, sliced\*** |

Sprinkle gelatin on ¼ cup cold water in the top part of a double boiler.

Place over boiling water until gelatin is completely dissolved.

Stir gelatin into lime juice and mayonnaise, and chill for 15 minutes.

Combine celery and cucumber in a medium-size bowl.

Gently mix in crabmeat.

Season with salt, paprika, and seafood seasoning.

Stir gelatin and blend into crabmeat.

Whip cream in a small bowl until stiff, and gently fold in with crabmeat mixture.

Pour mixture into an attractive buttered mold, and chill thoroughly until firm.

Unmold crabmeat on a bed of watercress.

Garnish with sliced olives.

---

\* Pimiento-stuffed olives, coarsely chopped may be used instead of pitted green olives for garnish. Sprinkle them over the mousse.

## Miss Laverne's Crab Imperial

1 cup mayonnaise (see recipe, page 99)

1 tablespoon Dijon mustard

1 teaspoon Worcestershire sauce

Dash of Tabasco sauce

1 small green papper, minced

1 small pimiento, finely chopped

1 teaspoon capers (optional)

½ teaspoon salt

Sprinkling of freshly ground black pepper

1 pound lump crabmeat

¼ cup dry, fine bread crumbs

2 tablespoons (¼ stick) butter, melted

Preheat oven to 350°.

Mix mayonnaise, mustard, Worcestershire, Tabasco, green pepper, pimiento, and (optional) capers in a medium-size bowl.

Season with salt and pepper.

Gently blend in crabmeat and mix lightly.

Spoon crabmeat mixture into 4 empty crab shells or 4 shell-shaped ovenproof dishes.

Sprinkle bread crumbs over crabmeat.

Drizzle melted butter over crumbs.

Place shells or dishes on a cookie sheet.

Bake for 15–20 minutes until bubbling and nicely browned.

## Jan's Snacking Crabmeat Spread

8 ounces cream cheese

1 teaspoon half-and-half

½ teaspoon Worcestershire sauce

½ pound backfin crabmeat

½ small onion, minced

½ teaspoon horseradish

½ teaspoon salt, or to taste

Sprinkling of white pepper

1 teaspoon sweet (unsalted) butter

¼ cup toasted almond slivers

Preheat oven to 350°.

Soften cream cheese with half-and-half and Worcestershire in a small bowl.

Blend in crabmeat, onion, horseradish, and mix lightly but well.

Season with salt and white pepper to taste.

Butter a small, attractive, ovenproof serving dish and fill with crab mixture.

Sprinkle toasted almond slivers over the top.

Bake for 15 minutes until crab mixture is heated through.

Serve hot right from the oven with assorted crackers, toasts, or other breads.

Keep crabmeat warm on a heated buffet tray.

## Mrs. Smedley-Moore's Crabmeat Supper

*(6 servings)*

| | |
|---|---|
| 1 small onion, minced | 1 teaspoon salt |
| 1 small green pepper, minced | ½ teaspoon celery salt |
| 6 tablespoons (¾ stick) butter | Generous sprinkling of freshly ground black pepper |
| 1 pound backfin crabmeat | Dash of Cayenne pepper |
| 3 medium–large potatoes, cooked, peeled, and diced | 4 eggs, well beaten |

Sauté onion and green pepper in butter in a medium-size heavy skillet until tender-crisp, approximately 2–3 minutes.

Add crabmeat and potatoes.

Season with salt, celery salt, pepper, and Cayenne.

Stir eggs gently into crab and potato mixture, and mix lightly but well.

Cover skillet and cook mixture over low heat, without stirring, for approximately 5 minutes or until set.

Cut in wedges and serve right from the skillet.

## Rosy Creamed Crabmeat

¼ pound large fresh mushrooms with stems, sliced

4 tablespoons (½ stick) butter

1 small onion, finely chopped

1 pound lump crabmeat

¼ cup dry sherry

1 cup heavy cream, warm

1 tablespoon tomato paste

Salt to taste

Sprinkling of white pepper

1 tablespoon brandy

Sauté mushrooms in butter in a large heavy skillet for approximately 5 minutes.

Stir in onion and continue cooking until golden, approximately 3 minutes.

Add crabmeat and sherry.

Blend cream and tomato paste gently into crab mixture.

Season with salt and pepper.

Continue cooking, stirring carefully so crabmeat doesn't break up, for approximately 1 minute, until mixture begins to thicken.

Thoroughly stir in brandy before serving hot on toast or rice.

# CRAB CAKES

## Cream Crab Cakes

1 egg

¼ cup heavy cream

½ teaspoon salt

Freshly ground black pepper
   to taste

1 pound lump crabmeat

1 tablespoon all-purpose flour

6 tablespoons (¾ stick) butter

1 tablespoon corn oil

Whisk egg, cream, salt, and pepper in a medium-size bowl.

Add crabmeat, sprinkle with flour, and mix lightly but well.

Heat butter and oil in a large, heavy skillet until just sizzling.

Drop tablespoonfuls of crabmeat into the skillet and fry for 3–4 minutes on each side until cakes are golden brown.

Remove crab cakes from skillet and dry on absorbent paper.

Serve immediately.


## Hilda's Madison Crab Cakes

1 egg

2 tablespoons mayonnaise (see
   recipe, page 99)

½ teaspoon dry mustard, or
   1 teaspoon prepared yellow
   mustard

Pinch of Cayenne pepper

Dash of Tabasco sauce

½ teaspoon salt

Generous sprinkling of
   freshly ground black pepper

1 pound backfin crabmeat

1 tablespoon fresh parsley,
   minced

4–5 saltine crackers, finely
   crumbled

4 tablespoons (½ stick) butter

4 tablespoons corn oil

Whisk egg, mayonnaise, mustard, Cayenne, Tabasco, salt, and pepper in a large bowl until smooth and creamy.

Add crabmeat, parsley, and cracker crumbs.

Toss mixture lightly but well.

Form crabmeat into 8 patties approximately ½ an inch thick.

Wrap patties in waxed paper and refrigerate for 1 hour.

Heat butter and oil in a large heavy skillet until just sizzling.

Fry crab cakes, turning once, approximately 5 minutes on each side, until golden brown and crispy.

Remove crab cakes from skillet and dry on absorbent paper.

Serve immediately.

## *Crabby Burgers*

*(4–6 servings)*

2 pounds backfin crabmeat

⅔ cup dry fine bread crumbs

⅔ cup mayonnaise (see recipe, page 99)

1 egg, well beaten

2 tablespoons horseradish

1 small onion, minced

1 small green pepper, minced

1 small stalk celery, minced

1 teaspoon prepared yellow mustard

1 teaspoon salt

Generous sprinkling of freshly ground black pepper

4 cups corn oil*

Mix all ingredients except oil in a large bowl.

Toss mixture lightly but well to blend thoroughly.

Heat corn oil in a large heavy skillet or Dutch oven. A piece of bread dropped into the oil will turn golden brown when the temperature of the oil is just right.

Form crabmeat into 12 patties approximately ½ an inch thick.

Fry crab patties until golden brown, 6–8 minutes.

Remove crab patties from skillet or Dutch oven with tongs, and dry on absorbent paper.

Serve immediately.

---

* Oil may be strained, refrigerated in a tightly covered container, and used again (but only for crab cakes or other crab dishes).

## Oxford Crab Cakes

1 pound backfin crabmeat

½ teaspoon salt

Freshly ground black pepper to taste

8 tablespoons (1 stick) butter

1 tablespoon fresh lemon juice

1 egg, slightly beaten

1 tablespoon Worcestershire sauce

1 hard-cooked egg, finely chopped

1 cup soft, white bread crumbs (2 slices)

¼ cup corn oil

Put crabmeat in a medium-size bowl and season with salt and pepper.

Melt butter in a small saucepan and stir in lemon juice, egg, and Worcestershire sauce. Pour over crabmeat.

Add chopped egg and bread crumbs, and mix lightly but well.

Form crabmeat into 8 patties approximately ½ inch thick.

In a large heavy skillet heat oil until just sizzling.

Fry crab cakes, turning once, about 5 minutes on each side until golden brown and crispy.

Remove crab cakes from skillet and dry on absorbent paper.

Serve immediately.

# SOFT-SHELL CRABS

Many people don't realize that soft-shell crabs are molting hard-shell blue crabs just after they've shed their hard shell. The "peeler" crabs (those which are about to molt) are put in "floats" or pens which are large and shallow rectangular boxes filled with constantly running water from the Bay. The crabs are watched closely and removed from the water within minutes after shedding their hard shell.

The soft-shell crab is considered a delicacy all over the world, and has a different flavor and texture from its hard-shell relative. No picking or cracking of shell and claws is necessary, since all of the firm white meat of the crab is eaten.

When buying soft-shell crabs, have them cleaned for you, or get an expert to do it dockside. It's a simple job but not a pleasant one if you're a bit squeamish.

## Sautéd Soft-Shell Crabs

8 soft-shell crabs, cleaned
¼–½ cup all-purpose flour
Salt

Freshly ground black pepper
8 tablespoons (1 stick) butter

Pat crabs dry with a paper towel.

Dust crabs with flour and sprinkle with salt and pepper.

Heat butter in a large heavy skillet until just sizzling.

Fry crabs for 3–5 minutes on each side, depending on size of crab, until crisp and nicely browned.

Remove crabs from skillet and dry on absorbent paper.

Lemon wedges are optional.

## Deep-Fried Soft-Shell Crabs

8 soft-shell crabs, cleaned
1 teaspoon salt
¾ cup dry, fine bread crumbs
¼ cup stone-ground white
  cornmeal

2 eggs
2 tablespoons milk
4 cups corn oil*

Pat crabs dry with a paper towel.

Sprinkle each crab with salt.

Thoroughly mix bread crumbs and cornmeal on waxed paper.

Whisk eggs with milk until well blended.

Heat oil in a large heavy skillet or Dutch oven. A piece of bread

---

* Oil may be strained, refrigerated in a tightly covered container, and used again (but only for crab dishes).

dropped into the oil will turn golden brown when the temperature of the oil is just right.

Dip each crab in egg and then into bread crumbs and cornmeal mixture, coating thoroughly on each side.

Fry crabs for 3–4 minutes until golden brown and crisp.

Remove crabs from skillet with tongs and dry on absorbent paper.

Fresh lemon juice may be sprinkled over crabs before serving.

# CRAB TIPS!

*(HARD)*

- Crabs should always be lively and clicking before you steam them.

- Steamed crabs should *never* come in contact with any surface or container that has held live crabs. Bacteria content from live crabs will cause contamination and spoilage of your cooked crabs.

- Leftover steamed crabs should cool at room temperature and be refrigerated within 3 hours after steaming.

- Always select a small heavy crab rather than a larger light one.

- Do-it-yourself crabbing in the Chesapeake is fun and easy, and you're allowed to take up to one bushel of crabs a day. You can use a long-handled net to dip up the crabs while you wade in the water or crab from a boat. Or you can tie bait to a line (chicken necks make good bait) and slowly pull in your crab when you feel a nibble on the line. Then it's a quick dip and the crab goes into the net. Collapsible crab traps are the lazy bones way of crabbing, but just as much fun. You simply secure your bait to the bottom of an open trap and wait until the unsuspecting crab enters to feed. You pull up the string on the trap and the sides close to catch the crab.

*(SOFT)*

- Soft-shell crabs should have pearly-gray translucent skin and plump, white underbellies with flesh that springs slightly to the touch. There should be no indication of hardening.

- Some cooks like to plunge the soft crab into boiling water for 1–2 seconds (until it just begins to turn pink) before sautéing.

FROM

OF THE

# THE WATERS

# CHESAPEAKE BAY:

# OYSTERS

INDIAN TRIBES must have been delighted when they first found large quantities of oysters along the coastline of the Chesapeake Bay. Here was an unlimited supply of succulent morsels of seafood, encased in a protective shell that could be used as both cooking utensil and server. Archaeologists have studied piles of shells, or "middens," on the Eastern Shore that are ample evidence of the Maryland Indians' fondness for oysters.

Almost since time began, the oyster has been eaten and appreciated by man. Celts harvested oysters and feasted on them regularly. The early Greeks cast their *votes* with oyster shells by making a mark on the pearly inside of the shell to indicate a choice of candidates—certainly a tasty way to cast a ballot! And Roman gourmands could devour five or six dozen oysters on the half-shell at dinner before proceeding with the next course.

In the 1800s oystering was a profitable business in Maryland, as it is today, and sometimes as many as twenty-five oyster boats would tie up at one time in an Eastern Shore port to unload their valuable cargo. Many of these oysters would be packed in ice and shipped by rail to various destinations (and gourmets) across the land, but the rest stayed in Maryland. No fine Eastern Shore dinner, whether for the president of the United States or a gentlemen's-club supper, would be complete without chilled oysters on the half-shell.

Oyster roasts were legend, and even though they were called "roasts" it was customary to serve no less than five different oyster dishes. A proper roast would include raw, fried, broiled, and of course roasted oysters, and a piping hot stew. A side dish was optional, and if anything it was usually mashed potatoes formed into patties and browned in butter.

If we were to re-create a typical oyster roast today, this is what we'd serve and how we would prepare the oysters. We'd also take two or three leisurely hours from both the nineteenth and twentieth centuries, so that we can properly enjoy this celebration of the oyster.

For an oyster roast for four:

**24 raw oysters, opened and on the deep half-shell (discard flat half-shell)**

**Oyster Stew Maryland***

**12 (half the recipe) Daddy Joe's Favorite Broiled Oysters***

**Eastern Shore Fried Oysters***

**24 roasted oysters**

The raw oysters on the half-shell should be chilled or well iced (unless they've just been taken from the Bay), and opened just before you serve them. Opening an oyster is easy but a bit tricky, and an inexpensive oyster knife is an absolute necessity. This is how it's done:

---

* See recipes, pages 83 and 29, respectively.

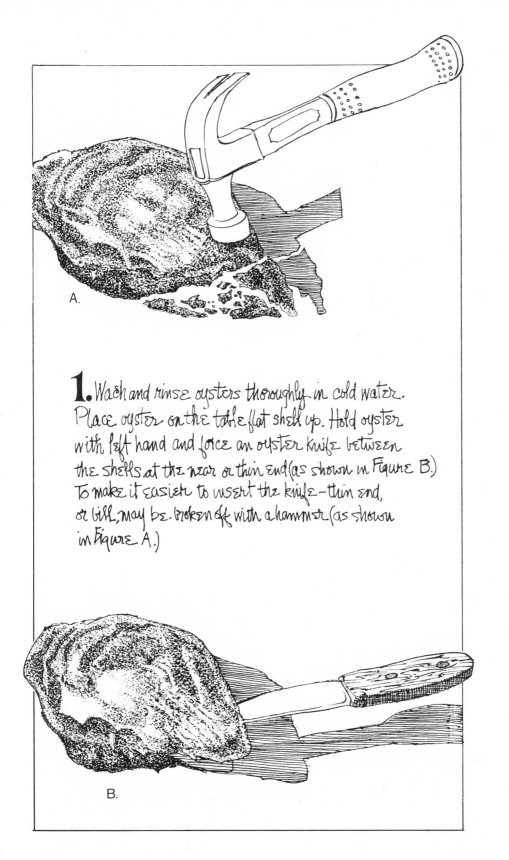

A.

**1.** Wash and rinse oysters thoroughly in cold water. Place oyster on the table flat shell up. Hold oyster with left hand and force an oyster knife between the shells at the near or thin end (as shown in Figure B.) To make it easier to insert the knife—thin end, or bill, may be broken off with a hammer (as shown in Figure A.)

B.

C.

**2.** Next, cut the large adductor muscle close to the flat upper shell in which it is attached and remove the shell (as shown in Figure c)

Small bowls of the oyster stew should be served piping hot within 15 minutes after the raw oysters. And then we rest for half an hour. The broiled oysters served next have just enough "fire" to whet the appetite for the golden brown and crispy fried oysters that follow, and the roast itself ends with the oysters for which it was named. We've allowed for 6 oysters per person, but you may want to increase the amount.

To roast oysters, preheat oven to 450 degrees. Place well-scrubbed oysters on a baking sheet or shallow pan for approximately 5 minutes until shells begin to open. Remove the top shell and serve oysters immediately. Individual metal trays are ideal for serving roasted, broiled, and raw oysters.

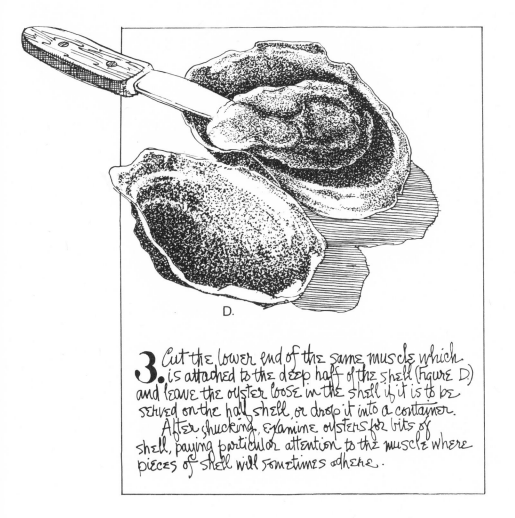

D.

**3.** Cut the lower end of the same muscle which is attached to the deep half of the shell (figure D) and leave the oyster loose in the shell if it is to be served on the half shell, or drop it into a container.

After shucking, examine oysters for bits of shell, paying particular attention to the muscle where pieces of shell will sometimes adhere.

On the side you'll want to have prepared and ready: lemons cut in small wedges; salt, and a pepper mill; a cruet of vinegar; the sauces included with the Eastern Shore Fried Oyster recipe (page 29); and oyster and saltine crackers. You'll also need forks, soup spoons, large napkins, and 4 good appetites!

Purists take their raw, broiled, and roasted oysters *plain*, and any concession would be a drizzling of either vinegar or fresh lemon juice over the oyster, with a sprinkling of freshly ground black pepper.

There are no set rules for condiments and sauces. The "rule" is what tastes good to you. We hope you'll enjoy preparing the "roast," and all the other oyster recipes in this section.

# THE RECIPES:

## Daddy Joe's Favorite
## Broiled Oysters

24 large oysters, opened, and
  on the deep half-shell
  (discard flat half-shell)

Worcestershire sauce

Hot sauce

2 strips bacon, minced

1 tablespoon fresh parsley,
  minced

Paprika

Preheat broiler for approximately 10 minutes.

Arrange oysters in a single layer on a cookie sheet.

Put 1–2 drops of Worcestershire and hot sauce on each oyster.

Top each oyster with bits of bacon.

Add a pinch of parsley on top of bacon, and a sprinkling of paprika.

Broil approximately 4 inches from heat until edges of oysters just begin to curl and bacon is crisp, 3–4 minutes.

Serve immediately.

## Eastern Shore Fried Oysters

1 pint shucked oysters,
  drained (oyster liquor may
  be reserved for another use)

1 cup all-purpose flour

1 cup dry fine bread crumbs

2 eggs

2 tablespoons light cream

1 teaspoon salt

Generous sprinkling of
  freshly ground black pepper

8 tablespoons (1 stick) butter

1 cup corn oil

Pat oysters dry with paper towels.

Thoroughly mix flour and bread crumbs on waxed paper.

Beat eggs with cream in a shallow dish.

Roll oysters in flour and bread crumb mixture, then in egg, and then in crumbs again, coating oysters thoroughly.

Season with salt and pepper.

Heat butter and oil in a large heavy skillet until just sizzling.

Reduce heat.

Fry oysters until nicely browned, 2–3 minutes on each side.

Remove oysters from skillet with tongs and dry on absorbent paper.

Serve immediately with lemon wedges, Chilled-and-Spicy Tomato Sauce, and Taylors Island Tartar Sauce (see recipes, pages 103 and 98).

## Lazy-Fried Oysters

1½–2 cups dry pancake mix

1 pint shucked oysters, drained (oyster liquor may be reserved for another use)

4 cups corn oil *

Salt to taste

Put pancake mix in a large bowl.

Add oysters, three or four at a time, and toss lightly until well coated with the pancake mix.

Put oysters in a wire basket and shake off excess mix.

Heat corn oil in a large heavy skillet or Dutch oven. A piece of bread dropped into the oil will turn golden brown when the temperature of the oil is just right.

Fry oysters until golden brown, 1½–2 minutes.

Remove from skillet or Dutch oven with tongs or a slotted spoon, and dry oysters on absorbent paper.

Season with salt to taste.

Serve immediately with lemon wedges, Chilled-and-Spicy Tomato Sauce, and Taylors Island Tartar Sauce (see recipes, pages 103 and 98).

---

* Oil may be strained, refrigerated in a tightly covered container, and used again (but only for fried oysters and other oyster dishes).

## Judy's Oyster Soufflé

1 pint shucked oysters, drained, with liquor reserved for later use

3 tablespoons butter

3 tablespoons all-purpose flour

½ cup oyster liquor

½ cup warm light cream

½ teaspoon salt

½ teaspoon white pepper

3 eggs, separated

1 tablespoon butter, softened

Preheat oven to 325°.

Pat oysters dry with paper towels.

Melt 3 tablespoons of butter in a medium-size heavy saucepan.

Add 3 tablespoons of flour and mix well with butter.

Measure out ½ cup oyster liquor, and reserve remaining liquor for another use.

Mix oyster liquor with cream, and slowly stir into butter and flour.

Continue cooking over low heat, whisking or stirring constantly, until sauce becomes thickened and smooth.

Remove from heat and mix oysters into sauce.

Season with salt and white pepper.

Separate egg yolks and set whites aside for later use.

Beat egg yolks well and stir into sauce.

Let sauce cool slightly for 2–3 minutes.

Butter sides and bottom of a 7″ ovenproof soufflé dish.

Beat egg whites until stiff, but not dry, and peaks form.

Fold egg whites carefully into oyster mixture.

Pour mixture into soufflé dish and bake for 30–35 minutes until firm.

Serve immediately.

## Oyster Puffs St. Michaels

1 pint shucked oysters, with
   liquor

½ cup oyster liquor

½ cup milk

4 tablespoons (½ stick) butter

2 teaspoons salt

½ teaspoon sugar

1 cup all-purpose flour

4 eggs

4 cups corn oil*

In a large heavy skillet, simmer oysters in their liquor until the edges just begin to curl.

Remove oysters from skillet with a slotted spoon and dry on absorbent paper.

Chop oysters fine and set aside.

Pour off oyster liquor and measure out ½ cup. Reserve any remaining liquor for another use.

Bring oyster liquor, milk, butter, salt, and sugar just to a boil in a medium-size heavy saucepan.

Reduce heat and add 1 cup flour.

Cook over low heat, stirring quickly and constantly, until mixture forms a smooth ball.

No flour or batter should stick to the sides of the saucepan.

Remove saucepan from heat and let batter cool slightly.

Add eggs, one at a time, and beat well after each egg is added.

Thoroughly mix chopped oysters into the batter.

Heat oil in a large heavy skillet or Dutch oven.

A piece of bread dropped into the oil will turn golden brown when the temperature of the oil is just right.

Drop batter into oil by tablespoonfuls and fry until golden brown, approximately 3–4 minutes. (Use teaspoonfuls of batter for tiny snacking or hors d'oeuvre puffs).

Turn puffs over with tongs as they brown.

---

* Oil may be strained, refrigerated in a tightly covered container, and used again (but only for fried oysters and other oyster dishes).

Remove puffs from oil and dry on absorbent paper.

Serve immediately with lemon wedges, Chilled-and-Spicy Tomato Sauce, and Taylors Island Tartar Sauce (see recipes, pages 103 and 98).

## Oysters Casino

3 slices bacon, coarsely chopped

1 small onion, finely chopped

1 small green pepper, finely chopped

1 small stalk celery, finely chopped

1 teaspoon fresh lemon juice

1 teaspoon fresh parsley, minced

1 teaspoon salt

Generous sprinkling of freshly ground black pepper

6 drops Worcestershire sauce

4 drops hot sauce

¼ teaspoon seafood seasoning

1 pint shucked oysters, drained (oyster liquor may be reserved for another use)

4–6 slices toast

Preheat oven to 400°.

Fry bacon in a small heavy skillet until almost crisp.

Add onion, green pepper, and celery and cook until vegetables are tender.

Stir in lemon juice, parsley, salt, pepper, Worcestershire, hot sauce, and seafood seasoning.

Arrange oysters in a single layer in a foil-lined, shallow baking dish.

Spread bacon mixture over oysters.

Bake for approximately 10 minutes until edges of oysters just begin to curl.

Serve immediately on toast.

# Oyster Kebabs

6 slices bacon, each cut in
    4 pieces

24 large shucked oysters,
    drained (oyster liquor may
    be reserved for another use)

4 ripe, firm, medium
    tomatoes, each cut in
    6 wedges

24 pimiento-stuffed olives

Freshly ground black pepper

Paprika

12 skewers

Preheat broiler for approximately 10 minutes.

Arrange 1 piece of bacon, 1 oyster, 1 tomato wedge, and 1 olive alternately on each skewer. Repeat so that skewers will hold 2 of each ingredient.

Sprinkle with freshly ground black pepper and paprika.

Arrange filled skewers in a single layer in a shallow baking dish.

Broil approximately 3 inches from heat until bacon is crisp, approximately 3 minutes.

Remove from broiler and serve immediately, 3 skewers for each person.

Note: Baked Rice in Chicken Broth (see recipe, page 68) is a good accompaniment for the kebabs.

# Oyster Skillet-Roast

*(4–6 servings)*

36 large shucked oysters,
    drained, with liquor
    reserved for later use

½ pound (2 sticks) butter,
    melted

Freshly ground black pepper

Line bottom of a large heavy skillet with oysters in a single layer.

Cook over low heat, turning 2 or 3 times carefully with tongs, until oysters brown a little and edges just begin to curl.

Pour off or spoon any oyster liquor (as it collects) from skillet, and add to drained liquor.

Measure out ¼ cup oyster liquor, and reserve remaining liquor for another use. Stir this liquor with butter in a small heavy saucepan until just sizzling.

Remove from heat and pour hot butter mixture into a chafing or other serving dish that will keep oysters warm while being served.

Sprinkle oysters with freshly ground black pepper.

Remove oysters from skillet with tongs and arrange in hot butter in the serving dish.

Note: Oysters may be spooned on toast points or served on small squares of toast.

## Scalloped Oysters

*(6 servings)*

1 tablespoon butter

4 cups crushed saltine crackers

1 quart shucked oysters, with liquor

4 tablespoons (½ stick) butter

Salt

Freshly ground black pepper

¼ cup chicken broth (see Basic Chicken Broth recipe, page 89)

¾–1¾ cups half-and-half

1 tablespoon fresh parsley, minced

Paprika

Preheat oven to 350°.

In a buttered 2-quart casserole, alternately layer cracker crumbs and oysters with liquor.

Dot each layer with butter and a sprinkling of salt and freshly ground black pepper.

Top layer should be cracker crumbs.

Pour chicken broth over cracker crumbs.

Add enough half-and-half (measurement varies because of the size of oysters and how saltines have been crushed) to barely cover casserole.

Sprinkle with parsley and paprika.

Bake oysters for 50–55 minutes until nicely browned.

Serve immediately.

## Charles Amos's Baked Oyster Sub

1 large loaf Italian or French bread

8 slices bacon

½ pint shucked oysters, drained (oyster liquor may be reserved for another use)

Sprinkling of all-purpose flour

1 small onion, minced

½ small green pepper, minced

2 medium–large tomatoes, sliced

Freshly ground black pepper

Preheat oven to 350°.

Cut bread in half and scoop out soft centers from each side of loaf to form a shell.

Fry bacon in a large heavy skillet until crisp.

Remove bacon from skillet with tongs and dry on absorbent paper.

Lightly sprinkle oysters with flour.

Fry oysters in bacon fat until nicely brown, approximately 1 minute on each side.

Remove oysters from skillet with tongs or a slotted spoon, and dry on absorbent paper.

Sauté onion and green pepper in skillet until tender-crisp, approximately 2 minutes.

Add a few drops of corn oil to the skillet if bacon fat has been absorbed.

Remove vegetables from skillet with a slotted spoon, and dry on absorbent paper.

Sauté tomato slices quickly in skillet, approximately half a minute on each side.

Remove tomatoes from skillet with a spatula, and dry on absorbent paper.

Layer bacon and oysters on half the bread.

Layer tomato slices and onion and green pepper mixture on other half of loaf, and season with freshly ground black pepper.

Press halves together and wrap bread in foil.

Bake for 15–20 minutes until bread is heated through. Remove foil.

Cut in 4 diagonal slices and serve immediately.

# Watermen's Oyster Pie

Prepare this flaky pie crust for pie, and set aside.

## FLAKY PIE CRUST

*(1 crust for 8- or 9-inch pie)*

**1½ cups all-purpose flour**
**½ teaspoon salt**
**8 tablespoons (1 stick) butter, softened**

**3 tablespoons cold water**
**Sprinkling of flour**

Sift flour and salt on a board.

Cut butter into flour with a fork or pastry blender, and mix well.

Gradually add just enough cold water to hold dough together.

Form dough into a ball.

Lightly flour board and roll dough out to ⅛–¼ inch thickness.

Cut dough for 8″ or 9″ pie approximately 1 inch wider all around and use this and any extra dough to fold under and press around the edges when pie is ready for baking.

24 large shucked oysters, with liquor

1 large onion, thinly sliced

4 small potatoes, peeled and thinly sliced

1 bay leaf

½ teaspoon salt

Generous sprinkling of freshly ground black pepper

Pinch of Cayenne pepper

2 tablespoons oyster liquor

½ cup warm half-and-half

1 Flaky Pie Crust (page 37)

Preheat oven to 450°.

Arrange alternate layers of oysters, onion slices, and potatoes in an 8"- or 9"-inch pie plate.

Place bay leaf in center of pie and season pie with salt, pepper, and Cayenne.

Measure out 2 tablespoons of oyster liquor, and reserve remaining liquor for another use.

Mix oyster liquor with half-and-half and pour over top of oyster filling.

Cover filling with dough and crimp edges around pie plate.

Prick top of dough several times with a fork.

Bake for approximately 15 minutes until crust of pie is golden brown.

Serve immediately.

# OYSTER TIPS!

- A fresh oyster has a tightly closed shell. Immediately discard any oyster with a gaping shell.

- Fresh oysters are pleasingly plump and have a healthy creamy color.

- Oyster liquor refrigerated in a tightly covered container for no more than one week may be used in stews, chowders, and other recipes that require oyster liquor.

- Freshly shucked oysters should be eaten as soon as possible for best flavor.

- Oysters are always served on the deep side of the half-shell, and the flat shell is discarded.

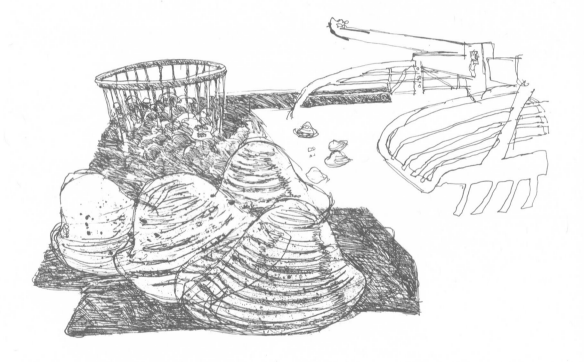

# THE WATERS

# CHESAPEAKE BAY:

# CLAMS

IF CRABS aren't steaming in kettles along the Eastern Shore, you're likely to find soft clams instead. These soft clams are called "manninose" in the Chesapeake Bay area, and they're distinguished by a protruding hoselike neck and an elongated, thin, and brittle shell. Delectable as these clams are, they're also sandy, and it's worth the time and effort to wash them very well before you serve them. Soft clams should be scrubbed with a stiff brush under cold running water, or in 4 or 5 changes of cold water. Put the clams in a large kettle and cover them with cold water. Add 1 tablespoon of salt and 1 cup of cornmeal to the kettle and "float" the clams for 4–6 hours. ("Floating" is really a misnomer, because any clam that rises to the surface should be immediately discarded along with any clam that has a broken or gaping shell.) Steamed clams and fried clams are equally popular in Maryland and so we've included recipes for both, plus a great clam appetizer that can double as a main course for 4 if you add a hearty salad.

## THE RECIPES:

EASY CLAM FRY
GOLDEN-FRIED CLAMS
HELAINE'S CLAM PRIX APPETIZER
EASTERN SHORE STEAMED CLAM FEAST

## Easy Clam Fry

1½–2 cups dry pancake mix

1 quart shucked soft-shell clams, drained (clam liquor may be reserved for another use)

4 cups corn oil*

Salt, to taste

Put pancake mix in a large bowl.

Add clams, three or four at a time, and toss lightly until well coated with pancake mix.

Put clams in a wire basket and shake off excess mix.

Heat corn oil in a large heavy skillet or Dutch oven. A piece of bread dropped into the oil will turn golden brown when the temperature of the oil is just right.

Fry clams until golden brown, approximately 1½–2 minutes.

Remove from skillet or Dutch oven with tongs or a slotted spoon, and dry clams on absorbent paper.

Season with salt to taste.

Serve immediately with lemon wedges, Chilled-and-Spicy Tomato Sauce, and Taylors Island Tartar Sauce (see recipes, pages 103 and 98).

## Golden-Fried Clams

1 quart shucked soft-shell clams, drained (clam liquor may be reserved for another use)

1 cup all-purpose flour

1 cup dry, fine bread crumbs

2 eggs

2 tablespoons light cream

1 teaspoon salt

Generous sprinkling of freshly ground black pepper

8 tablespoons (1 stick) butter

1 cup corn oil

Pat clams dry with paper towels.

---

* Oil may be strained, refrigerated in a tightly covered container, and used again (but only for fried clams and oter clam dishes).

Thoroughly mix flour and bread crumbs on waxed paper.

Beat eggs with cream in shallow dish.

Roll clams in flour and bread crumbs mixture, then in egg, and then in crumbs again, coating clams thoroughly.

Season with salt and pepper.

Heat butter and oil in a large heavy skillet until just sizzling.

Reduce heat.

Fry clams until nicely browned, approximately 2–3 minutes on each side.

Remove clams from skillet with tongs, and dry on absorbent paper.

Serve immediately with lemon wedges, Chilled-and-Spicy Tomato Sauce, and Taylors Island Tartar Sauce (see recipes, pages 103 and 98).

## Helaine's Clam Prix Appetizer

*(8 servings)*

1 medium clove garlic, minced

2 tablespoons (¼ stick) butter

¼ pound fresh mushrooms with stems, finely chopped

1 medium stalk celery, finely chopped

½ small green pepper, finely chopped

½ medium onion, finely chopped

1 pint shucked hard- or soft-shell clams with liquor, minced

½ cup dry, fine bread crumbs

2 tablespoons dry white wine (or a few drops more to taste)

Generous sprinkling of Parmesan or Romano cheese

Pinch of oregano

Pinch of basil

Salt, to taste

4 strips of bacon, cut in half

Preheat broiler for approximately 10 minutes.

Sauté garlic in butter in a medium-size heavy skillet for 2–3 minutes.

Add mushrooms, celery, green pepper, and onion and continue cooking until vegetables are tender-crisp.

Mix in clams and liquor and turn off heat.

Slowly stir in bread crumbs until all clam liquor is absorbed. Add more bread crumbs if necessary, but don't let the mixture become too thick.

Blend in wine, cheese, oregano, and basil.

Salt to taste.

Pile clam mixture onto 8 large scallop shells or scallop-shaped broilerproof dishes.

Top each shell with ½ strip of bacon.

Arrange shells/dishes on a cookie sheet and broil approximately 4 inches from heat until nicely browned and bacon is crisp, 3–4 minutes.

Remove from broiler and serve immediately.

Note: Lemon and lime wedges may be served with clams.

## Eastern Shore Steamed Clam Feast

6–8 dozen soft-shell clams, well scrubbed and in shell

(Allow 1½–2 dozen clams for each person)

1 large onion, coarsely chopped

1 teaspoon salt

Generous sprinkling of freshly ground black pepper

1 cup dry white wine

4 tablespoons (½ stick) butter

Water

1 pound butter

2–3 loaves fresh Italian or French bread

Place clams in a large kettle, steamer, or pot with a tight-fitting lid.

Sprinkle onion over top of clams and season with salt and freshly ground black pepper.

Pour wine over all and add butter.

Add enough water to pot to bring measure to approximately ½ inch.

Cover pot tightly and bring water to a boil.

Reduce heat and steam clams for 5–10 minutes until shells open.

Discard any clams that don't open.

Remove clams and shells with a slotted spoon to a large serving bowl, or individual bowls if you prefer.

Strain clam broth and taste for additional seasoning.

Reheat clam broth if necessary, and serve hot in 4 individual bowls.

Melt butter in a small heavy saucepan until just sizzling, and pour into 4 individual bowls.

Dip each clam into broth, then into butter, then into mouth.

Crusty French or Italian bread, warmed for a few minutes in the oven, is ideal for dipping into remaining clam broth and butter.

# FROM THE
# CHESAPEAKE BAY:

# WATERS OF THE FISH—THE CATCH OF THE DAY

A WIDE VARIETY of fish are plentiful year round on the Eastern Shore, whether on the docks, in the markets, or there for the taking at the end of your own fishing pole. If you're feeling sporting you can always enter one of the many fishing contests that are held during the year and are open to all. Aside from the prizes and the trophies that are awarded, the biggest catches of the day usually mean a fish fry—and *everyone* is invited!

*Fresh* is the most important word when you're preparing any recipe that includes fish and, although you may not be able to see your fish actually taken out of the water, there are five basic things to look for:

- A fresh fish will have bright, clear, and bulging eyes.

- The gills will be a healthy-looking reddish pink, with no trace of stickiness.

- The scales will adhere closely to the skin and retain their colorful sheen.

- Flesh should be firm and elastic to the touch, and cling to the bones.

- Although all fish have some natural odor, you should never be able to detect an *unpleasant* odor.

We prefer to leave the cleaning of fish to the experts, but you can invest in a sharp knife and one of many fine books and pamphlets that show you how to do the job yourself. And then there are the fishermen/women who swear that fish taste better if you clean your own catch. Fish are cleaned and dressed in several ways.

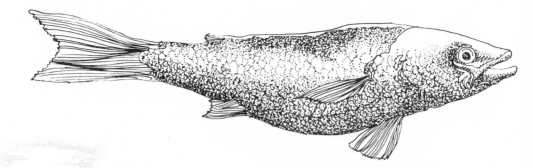

*WHOLE fish—as they come from the water.*

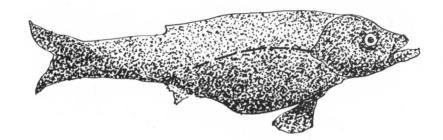

*DRAWN fish—scaled and split with entrails removed.*

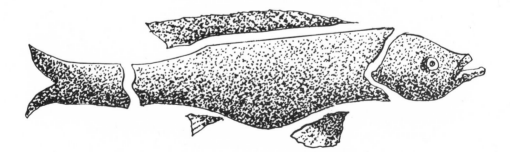

*DRESSED fish—scaled and split with entrails, head, tail, and fins removed. Sometimes the backbone is also removed.*

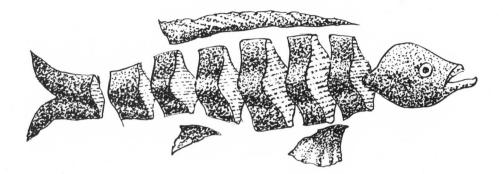

STEAKS—cross-section slices from
larger dressed fish, cut 1 inch or more thick.

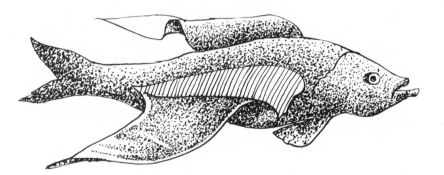

FILLETS—boneless sides of the
fish cut lengthwise away from the backbone,
and may be skinned.

BUTTERFLY (DOUBLE) FILLETS—two
boneless sides of the fish cut lengthwise away
from the backbone and held together
by the uncut flesh of the belly.
They may be skinned.

# THE RECIPES:

SHERIFF DAN'S BAKED WHOLE ROCKFISH (STRIPED
   BASS)
PAN-FRIED SPOT
GOLDEN-FRIED SEA SQUAB
   (BLOWFISH/TOADFISH/PUFFER)
INDIVIDUAL FLOUNDER FILLETS IN CRUST
PERCH FILLETS IN FIREHOUSE TOMATO SAUCE
OVEN-STEAMED "BONELESS" SAVORY SHAD
SUSAN'S BAKED BLUEFISH WITH CAPER STUFFING
HERBED-AND-SPICED BROILED BLUEFISH FILLETS

## Sheriff Dan's Baked Whole Rockfish (Striped Bass)

*(6 servings)*

1 tablespoon butter

1 whole rockfish (3–3½ pounds), dressed

Salt

Freshly ground black pepper

2 tablespoons (¼ stick) butter

3 slices bacon

2–3 lemons, cut in wedges

Preheat oven to 325°.

Butter a baking dish large enough to hold rockfish with basting juices.

Dry rockfish thoroughly inside and out.

Sprinkle inside of fish with salt and pepper, and dot with butter.

Place fish on its side in baking dish.

Lay strips of bacon across top.

Bake for approximately 10 minutes per pound, until fish flakes easily with a fork.

Baste 2 or 3 times during baking.

Remove rockfish to a prewarmed platter and spoon cooking juices over top.

Serve immediately with lemon wedges.

Note: Small, whole boiled potatoes are traditionally served with the baked rockfish.

## Pan-Fried Spot

4 whole spot (about ½ pound each), drawn

½ teaspoon salt

Freshly ground black pepper

½ cup stone-ground white cornmeal

½ cup half-and-half

8 tablespoons (1 stick) butter

Rosemary

4 sprigs fresh parsley, coarsely chopped

Wipe spot with damp cloth.

Lightly sprinkle inside of each fish with salt and freshly ground black pepper.

Spread cornmeal out on waxed paper.

Dip each fish in half-and-half and then in cornmeal.

Heat butter in a medium-size heavy skillet until just sizzling.

Reduce heat.

Fry spot until golden brown on one side, approximately 5 minutes.

Sprinkle each fish with rosemary, and turn carefully with spatula.

Fry spot on other side approximately 5 minutes, until fish is golden brown and flakes easily with a fork.

Serve immediately on prewarmed plates.

Sprinkle with parsley before serving.

Note: Lemon wedges may be served with fish.

## Golden-Fried Sea Squab (Blowfish/Toadfish/Puffer)

| | |
|---|---|
| 8 sea squab, dressed | 1 cup finely crushed unsalted cracker crumbs |
| ½ teaspoon salt | |
| Freshly ground black pepper | ½ cup half-and-half |
| ½ cup stone-ground yellow cornmeal | 1 cup corn oil |
| | 2 lemons, cut in wedges |

Wipe sea squab with damp cloth.

Sprinkle with salt and freshly ground black pepper.

Thoroughly mix cornmeal and cracker crumbs on waxed paper.

Dip fish in half-and-half and then in cornmeal and cracker crumbs.

Heat oil in a medium-size heavy skillet until just sizzling.

Reduce heat. Fry fish for 3 minutes on one side until golden brown.

Turn fish carefully with a slotted spoon or tongs and fry for 2 minutes on the other side until golden brown.

Remove from skillet and dry on absorbent paper.

Serve immediately with lemon wedges.

## Individual Flounder Fillets in Crust

4 flounder fillets (about
   ¼ pound each)

1 egg

1 tablespoon light cream

½ teaspoon salt

Generous sprinkling of
   freshly ground black pepper

Pinch of paprika

½ cup all-purpose flour

½ cup corn oil

4 large plain or seeded, hard
   club rolls (or small sub/hero
   hard rolls)

1 small sweet pickle, minced

1 small onion, minced

2 teaspoons prepared yellow
   mustard

3 tablespoons mayonnaise (see
   recipe, page 99)

1 large ripe tomato, coarsely
   chopped and drained

1 tablespoon butter, melted

Preheat oven to 350°.

Wipe flouder fillets with damp cloth.

Beat egg with cream in a small bowl.

Mix salt, freshly ground black pepper, and paprika into flour on waxed paper.

Dip fillets in egg and then in flour.

Heat oil in a medium-size heavy skillet until just sizzling.

Reduce heat.

Fry fish for 2–3 minutes on each side until golden brown.

Remove fish from skillet and dry on absorbent paper.

Split rolls in half and scoop out soft centers from each side of rolls to make a shell.

Thoroughly mix pickle, onion, mustard, and mayonnaise in a small bowl.

Spread mixture on each half of rolls. Then place a fish fillet on each roll.

Spoon chopped tomatoes over fish fillets.

Press halves together and brush rolls with melted butter.

Wrap rolls in foil and bake for 10 minutes until heated through.

Remove foil and serve immediately.

## Perch Fillets in
## Firehouse Tomato Sauce

*(6 servings)*

| | |
|---|---|
| 1 large onion, coarsely chopped | 2 large ripe tomatoes, peeled and coarsely chopped |
| 4 tablespoons (½ stick) butter | ½ cup dry white wine |
| 1 tablespoon corn oil | 1 bay leaf |
| 1 large clove garlic, minced | 1 tablespoon fresh parsley, minced |
| 1 large stalk celery with leaves, coarsely chopped | Salt |
| 1 medium green pepper, coarsely chopped | Freshly ground black pepper |
| 1 medium carrot, finely chopped | 2 pounds white perch fillets, cut in serving pieces |
| 1 cup tomato sauce | |

Sauté onion in butter and oil in a medium-size heavy skillet until golden.

Add garlic, celery, green pepper, and carrot and cook until tender-crisp.

Stir in tomato sauce, chopped tomatoes, wine, bay leaf, and parsley.

Season with salt and freshly ground black pepper to taste.

Simmer sauce for 1 hour, stirring occasionally.

Preheat oven to 350°.

Wipe perch fillets with a damp cloth.

Oil a shallow baking dish large enough to hold fillets in a single layer.

Arrange fillets in baking dish and pour tomato sauce over them.

Bake for approximately 25 minutes, until fish flakes easily with a fork.

Serve immediately, piping hot.

Note: Fish and sauce may be spooned over plain rice.

## Oven-Steamed "Boneless" Savory Shad

*(6 servings)*

1 whole shad (3–4 pounds), dressed

Salt

Freshly ground black pepper

1 cup dry white wine

Water

1 large stalk celery (with leaves), coarsely chopped

1 medium carrot, coarsely chopped

1 medium onion, coarsely chopped

1 tablespoon fresh parsley, minced

1 large clove garlic, minced

2 bay leaves

Preheat oven to 300°.

Dry shad thoroughly inside and out.

Sprinkle fish inside and out with salt and freshly ground black pepper.

Place fish on its side in a roasting pan with a rack and a *tight*-fitting cover.

Pour wine into pan.

Add enough water to bring liquid level just under the rack holding shad (approximately 3–4 cups).

Sprinkle celery, carrot, onion, parsley, and garlic over fish and add bay leaves.

Cover pan *tightly* and steam in the oven for 5 hours.

Baste shad frequently while steaming.

Remove fish to a prewarmed platter and spoon cooking juices over top.

Note: Shad bones will be soft enough to eat as long as the pan cover fits *tightly* and fish is steamed for full 5 hours.

# Susan's Baked Bluefish with Caper Stuffing

*(6 servings)*

## STUFFING

2 cups soft bread crumbs

1 tablespoon butter, melted

2 tablespoons capers

1 small dill pickle, minced

1 tablespoon fresh parsley, minced

1 small slice of onion, minced

Pinch of seafood seasoning (optional)

Salt to taste

Freshly ground black pepper to taste

½ cup boiling water

## FISH

1 whole bluefish (4½– 5 pounds), dressed

Salt

Freshly ground black pepper

1 tablespoon butter, melted

½ cup boiling water

1 large slice of onion

Preheat oven to 350°.

Mix all stuffing ingredients except water in a medium-size bowl.

Slowly add water and blend thoroughly into bread crumbs mixture.

Dry bluefish thoroughly inside and out.

Lightly sprinkle inside of fish with salt and pepper.

Stuff bluefish *loosely* with bread crumbs mixture and close with skewers.

Brush fish with melted butter and place on its side in a baking dish.

Pour ½ cup boiling water into dish and add onion slice.

Bake bluefish for approximately 50 minutes or until fish flakes easily with a fork.

Remove fish to a prewarmed platter and take out skewers.

Serve immediately.

# Herbed-and-Spiced Broiled Bluefish Fillets

3 tablespoons corn oil

1 tablespoon fresh lime juice

1–2 drops hot sauce

1–2 drops Worcestershire sauce

1 medium clove garlic, minced

½ small onion, minced

1 tablespoon fresh parsley, minced

1 tablespoon Dijon mustard

t teaspoon paprika

1 teaspoon fennel seeds, crushed

1 teaspoon salt, or to taste

Generous sprinkling of freshly ground black pepper

4 bluefish fillets

Thoroughly mix all ingredients except fish in a shallow dish large enough to hold bluefish fillets in a single layer.

Add fish and coat well on both sides, rubbing mixture lightly into the fillets.

Cover and let stand 1 hour.

Before broiling, preheat broiler for 10 minutes.

Broil fillets skin side down approximately 2 inches from heat for 5–6 minutes.

Baste fish once during broiling and do not turn.

Serve immediately on prewarmed plates.


# FISH TIPS!

- Fish should not be rinsed under running water but dipped in cold, salted water and patted dry with paper towels.

- Handle fish carefully since bruised and punctured skin and flesh will deteriorate rapidly.

- If you don't use a fresh fish immediately, wrap it in waxed or other moisture-proof paper and store under ice (or in the coldest part of your refrigerator) until ready to cook.

- Rub slightly moistened salt on cooking utensils and rinse with hot water to remove any fish odor.

# EVERY DAY . . .
# AND SUNDAY

SUNDAY DINNER in many Eastern Shore homes is still the traditional chicken. A plump, juicy bird roasted to golden brown perfection with all the good trimmings of stuffing, fluffy mashed potatoes with cream gravy, greens cooked tender with a thin slab of salt pork, and hot biscuits with butter that often come to the table homemade. Or perhaps, more informally, there will be a heaping platterful of fried chicken, crunchy-crisp on the outside and moist and tender on the inside, served up with homemade potato salad and crisp 'slaw just waiting to be packed into a picnic basket for a day on the Chesapeake. No doubt about it, Marylanders love their chicken on Sunday and any other day—and with good reason. Some of the finest birds in the world are raised on the Eastern Shore.

Every Sunday morning about ten o'clock one of our neighbors, Miss Hilda (who is famous throughout the Eastern Shore for her skill with fried chicken), wraps a big white apron around her waist and begins frying what seems like an endless assortment of thighs, legs, breasts, and wings. She says there's just no sense in frying chicken if you're not going to make a big platterful or two to share with friends and relatives who might drop in, and you can be sure they always do!

That unmistakable and tempting aroma of chicken sizzling in a skillet can be sniffed out and detected a country mile downwind of any kitchen. The fried chicken recipes that follow have been made purposely generous to allow for both company and good appetites, and with luck you may even have a few leftover pieces.

For frying the chickens, Miss Hilda uses corn oil and shortening, or a combination of corn oil and a slab of lean salt pork (appropriately called "streak o' lean") cut in small pieces. Sometimes she fries the chickens in bacon fat with a little corn oil added, and the leftover thick slices of crisp bacon are broken up and set aside to eat later with the chicken. The chickens are always cut in "comfortable" small pieces that are easy to eat, with the skin intact, and oil and fat in the skillet are never more than ½ inch deep. Miss Hilda also believes that all great fried chicken begins with a large, heavy, cast-iron skillet, the kind that is still called a "spider" in some homes. In early days this type of skillet was mounted on legs for cooking directly over a fire and, crouched above the heat, it resembled a large black spider. Some imaginative cook noticed the resemblance, and the skillet got its nickname. You may have your own favorite skillet and prefer to use it, but in Maryland the traditional and respected pan for frying chicken is this well-seasoned "spider."

Heavy brown-paper bags are kept handy for shaking up the chicken pieces in flour, and later the paper bags or sheets of brown paper are spread out for drying the chicken as it comes from the skillet. Miss Hilda never looks at a clock, but her chicken stays in the skillet no more than 20–25 minutes, and she covers the pan during the last 10 minutes of frying. The chicken is turned twice with a fork (or tongs may be used).

Perfect fried chicken takes practice, and don't be afraid to experiment with ingredients. Shortening; lard; butter; salt pork; bacon; corn, peanut, and other oils all should be tried in various combinations until you find the mixture that "fries" best for you. Those "secret" recipes that have been developed by master chefs, or handed down through generations of families, can be as near as your spice shelf and your imagination. Why not a good pinch of cinnamon, nutmeg, curry powder, Cayenne, or any one of your favorite spices mixed into the flour you're using to coat the chicken? Or try a dash of Worcestershire, Tabasco, fresh lemon juice, or even the favorite "secret" ingredient of one chef—a few drops of almond extract mixed into the batter.

Adventurous testing is the only way to create *any* recipe for your own taste, and you'll be joining a long list of distinguished cooks who have invented superb and classic dishes through trial and (only occasionally!) error.

If we seem to be neglecting those of you who don't like your chicken fried, please turn the page. We've collected some other very special chicken recipes from Eastern Shore kitchens and we hope you'll test, taste, improvise if you like, but most of all—enjoy them.

# THE RECIPES:

## Eastern Shore Chicken and "Slipperies"

| | |
|---|---|
| 1 whole chicken (about 3½ pounds) | 1 large onion, coarsely chopped |
| 1½ teaspoons salt | 1 large carrot, coarsely chopped |
| Generous sprinkling of freshly ground black pepper | 1 large stalk of celery (with leaves), finely chopped |
| 1 tablespoon fresh parsley, minced | 2 quarts water |

Place chicken in a large heavy kettle or Dutch oven.

Sprinkle chicken with salt and freshly ground black pepper.

Add parsley, onion, carrot, and celery to chicken.

Pour water over all.

Cover kettle or Dutch oven and bring water to a boil.

Reduce heat and simmer chicken and vegetables for about 1 hour until chicken is fork-tender.

Remove chicken from broth and set aside.

## "SLIPPERIES"

| | |
|---|---|
| 2 cups all-purpose flour | ¾ cup hot water |
| ½ teaspoon salt | Sprinkling of flour |
| 2 teaspoons vegetable shortening | |

Sift flour and salt together in a large bowl.

Add vegetable shortening and stir in hot water.

Work mixture with hands into a soft dough.

Lightly flour a board and roll out dough with a rolling pin until very thin. The secret of these "slipperies" is a *thin* dough (about ⅟₁₆ inch) so just keep rolling!

Cut dough into rectangular pieces, large or small depending on your preference.

Sprinkle dough pieces lightly with flour.

Bring chicken broth to a boil.

Add a little more water to the broth if necessary.

Drop the dough into boiling broth, and reduce heat to medium-high.

Continue cooking, stirring often with a wooden spoon, until "slipperies" sink.

Remove and discard skin from the chicken.

Cut chicken into serving pieces and serve with "slipperies" and broth/gravy on the side. Or, cut the chicken into bite-size pieces and add them to the "slipperies" and broth/gravy.

Season to taste.

## Honey-Butter Dipped Chicken

4 tablespoons (½ stick) butter, melted

½ cup warm honey

¼ cup prepared yellow mustard

1 teaspoon salt

Sprinkling of white pepper

1 chicken (3–3½ pounds), cut in serving pieces

Preheat oven to 375°.

Thoroughly mix melted butter, warm honey, mustard, salt, and white pepper in a shallow baking dish large enough to hold chicken pieces in a single layer.

Use tongs to coat both sides of chicken pieces generously with honey-butter mixture.

Bake chicken skin side down for 30 minutes. Turn chicken with tongs and baste. Bake skin side up for 30 minutes more.

Baste chicken again and serve immediately.

# Chicken and Vegetables Tossed in a Skillet*

2 large, whole chicken breasts, skinned, boned, and cut in bite-size pieces

1 tablespoon cornstarch

1 tablespoon vegetable oil

3 tablespoons soy sauce

Generous sprinkling of freshly ground black pepper

1 tablespoon vegetable oil

1 bunch fresh broccoli (about 1 pound) flowerets separated and stalks cut in 1–1½-inch pieces

½ pound fresh mushrooms with stems, sliced

6 green onions (scallions) with tops, cut in 1-inch pieces

2 medium–large tomatoes, each cut in 8 wedges

Prepare chicken breasts and set aside.

Mix cornstarch, 1 tablespoon vegetable oil, and soy sauce in a shallow dish large enough to hold chicken.

Sprinkle generously with freshly ground black pepper.

Whisk for a few seconds until well blended.

Add chicken pieces and coat well with the mixture.

Cover chicken and refrigerate overnight.

Heat 1 tablespoon vegetable oil in a large heavy skillet until *just* sizzling.

Add chicken to the skillet and toss quickly until brown, for about 5 minutes.

Remove chicken and set aside.

Add broccoli to the skillet (be sure any tough parts of the stalks have been peeled away) and toss quickly for about 2 minutes.

Add mushrooms and green onions to the skillet.

Continue cooking until green onions are tender-crisp, for about 3 minutes.

---

* Overnight Recipe

Return chicken to the skillet, and top with tomato wedges.

Cover skillet and continue cooking for about 2 minutes.

Toss chicken and vegetables lightly but well and serve immediately.

## *Chicken Fritters**

1½–2 cups cooked chicken, cut in small pieces (almost minced)

1 teaspoon salt

Generous sprinkling of freshly ground black pepper

1 teaspoon fresh parsley, minced

1 lemon (juice)

1¼ cups all-purpose flour

Pinch of salt

2 teaspoons baking powder

1 egg, beaten

⅔ cup milk

4 cups corn oil**

Toss chicken lightly but well in a bowl with salt, pepper, parsley, and juice from lemon.

Set aside and let chicken mixture stand for 1 hour.

Combine flour, pinch of salt, baking powder, egg, and milk in a large bowl and whisk until thoroughly mixed.

Stir chicken mixture into batter and blend well.

Heat oil in large heavy kettle or Dutch oven. A piece of bread dropped into the oil will turn golden brown when the temperature of the oil is just right. *Never let the oil start to smoke.*

Drop batter by tablespoonfuls into oil and fry until golden brown, approximately 2–3 minutes.

Remove chicken fritters from oil with a slotted spoon and dry on absorbent paper.

Serve fritters immediately on a prewarmed platter with Chilled-and-Spicy Tomato Sauce (see recipe, page 103) on the side.

---

* Good recipe for leftovers

** Oil may be strained, refrigerated in a tightly covered container, and used again (but *only* for chicken or more chicken fritters).

## Herb-Baked Chicken in Cream

¼ cup all-purpose flour

1 teaspoon salt

Generous sprinkling of
   freshly ground black pepper

1 teaspoon celery salt

Pinch of Cayenne

1 teaspoon fresh parsley,
   minced

1 chicken (about 3½ pounds),
   cut in serving pieces

1 cup heavy cream

Preheat oven to 350°.

Thoroughly mix flour, seasonings, and parsley.

Dredge chicken on all sides with flour mixture.

Place chicken pieces in a 2½-quart ovenproof casserole with a tight-fitting cover.

Pour cream over the chicken.

Cover casserole and bake for approximately 50 minutes, or until chicken is fork-tender.

Remove cover from casserole and bake chicken for 15 minutes more.

## Big George's Boneless Fried Chicken

5 whole chicken breasts,
   skinned, boned, and cut in
   small serving pieces

3 eggs

1 cup milk

1 teaspoon salt

Generous sprinkling of
   freshly ground black pepper

1 teaspoon poultry seasoning

1 box (12 ounces) cornflakes,
   finely crushed

½ box (10 ounces) Bisquick

2 cups peanut oil

2 lemons (juice)

Prepare chicken pieces and set aside.

Thoroughly beat eggs with milk, salt, pepper, and poultry seasoning in a bowl or casserole dish large enough to hold the chicken.

Soak chicken in milk mixture and refrigerate for 2 hours.

Mix finely crushed cornflakes and Bisquick in a large plastic bag.

Shake thoroughly and continue crushing and mixing until texture is a "beige-and-white tweed."

Put the chicken, a few pieces at a time, into the bag and generously coat each piece with the mixture. When all pieces have been thoroughly coated, refrigerate chicken again for two hours.

Heat peanut oil in a large heavy skillet. A piece of bread dropped into the oil will turn golden brown when the temperature of the oil is just right.

Fry chicken approximately 4 minutes on each side, turning once with tongs.

Remove chicken pieces from the skillet with tongs and dry on absorbent paper.

Sprinkle lemon juice over chicken before serving.

## Grilled Chicken "Shoestrings" with Baked Rice in Chicken Broth*

2 large whole chicken breasts, skinned, boned, and pounded flat to about ½ an inch

¼ cup soy sauce

2 teaspoons peanut oil

2 tablespoons sugar

1 small onion, minced

1 large clove garlic, minced

Dash of Tabasco sauce

Generous sprinkling of freshly ground black pepper

2 tablespoons sesame seeds

Prepare chicken breasts and cut in strips 4 inches long and ½–¾ inches wide. Set aside.

Combine all ingredients in a shallow broiler-proof dish large enough to hold chicken in a single layer.

Whisk mixture for a few seconds until well blended.

———————

* Overnight recipe

Add chicken strips, cover dish, and refrigerate overnight.

Remove chicken from refrigerator 30 minutes before broiling.

Spoon marinade over the strips.

Preheat broiler for 5 minutes.

Broil chicken strips for approximately 4 minutes on each side, turning once with tongs, until brown. Baste with marinade once or twice during broiling.

Serve with Baked Rice in Chicken Broth.


## BAKED RICE IN CHICKEN BROTH

Note: Prepare and bake rice after chicken strips have been removed from the refrigerator.

1 medium onion, coarsely
  chopped

4 tablespoons (½ stick) butter

1 cup raw rice

2 cups boiling chicken broth
  (see Basic Chicken Broth
  recipe, page 89)

1 tablespoon butter, melted

1 tablespoon warm heavy
  cream

Preheat oven to 375°.

Sauté onion in butter in medium-size ovenproof casserole, with a tight-fitting cover, until golden.

When onion is golden, stir in rice and coat well.

Mix in boiling chicken broth.

Cover casserole and bake for 20–25 minutes.

Combine melted butter and warm cream, and gently stir into rice before serving.

## Big Old Chicken Barbecue in the Oven

4 large, whole chicken breasts

1 large onion, cut in 8 slices

Paprika

1½ cups tomato juice

1 bay leaf

2 large cloves garlic, minced

1½ teaspoon salt

Generous sprinkling of freshly ground black pepper

Pinch of dry mustard

1 teaspoon sugar

1½ tablespoon Worcestershire sauce

¾ cup cider vinegar

Dash of Tabasco sauce

Pinch of red pepper flakes

2 tablespoons (¼ stick) butter, melted

Preheat oven to 300°.

Place chicken breasts skin side up in a shallow baking dish.

Tuck a slice of onion under each side of breast.

Sprinkle chicken breasts with paprika.

Thoroughly combine all other ingredients in a medium-size bowl. Pour mixture over the chicken.

Bake for 1½ hours, basting occasionally with the sauce.

Note: This dish may be made a day ahead and reheated before serving.

## Savory Roast Chicken with Corn Pone Stuffing

*(6 servings)*

1 whole roasting chicken (4½–5 lb.)

1 tablespoon vegetable oil

Corn Pone Stuffing

Coarsely woven clean white cloth (such as cheesecloth) soaked in vegetable oil to cover chicken

Salt

Freshly ground black pepper

# CORN PONE STUFFING

Note: Prepare corn pone before roasting chicken.

3 eggs, well beaten

2 cups buttermilk

3 tablespoons butter, melted

2 teaspoons salt

2½ cups stone-ground white cornmeal

3 teaspoons baking powder

1 teaspoon baking soda

1 tablespoon hot water

1 medium onion, minced

1 medium stalk celery, minced

1 small green pepper, minced

1 teaspoon fresh parsley, minced

1 tablespoon poultry seasoning

2 tablespoons hot water

Salt to taste

Sprinkling of freshly ground black pepper

Pinch of Cayenne

Preheat oven to 425° (increase to 450° before roasting chicken).

Thoroughly blend eggs, buttermilk, butter, and salt in a large bowl.

Sift cornmeal and baking power together, and then slowly stir into the eggs-buttermilk mixture.

Whisk to make a thick batter, adding more cornmeal if necessary.

Dissolve baking soda in 1 tablespoon of hot water and add to batter.

Mix well and pour batter into a shallow, greased baking pan.

Bake for 25–30 minutes until corn pone browns.

Remove corn pone from oven and let cool. Break the corn pone into small pieces and crumble thoroughly.

In a large bowl combine corn pone, onion, celery, green pepper, parsley, poultry seasoning, hot water, salt, pepper, and Cayenne.

Toss stuffing lightly but well. Add more hot water if stuffing is too dry.

Preheat oven to 450°.

Wash chicken thoroughly inside and out with cold water. Pat dry inside and out with a paper towel.

Rub chicken all over with vegetable oil.

Stuff bird lightly (bake leftover stuffing in a separate dish, or see "Chicken Tips" on page 77).

Truss with small skewers and/or twine (nothing fancy).

Cover surface of chicken with cloth that has been soaked in vegetable oil.

Place chicken on rack in an uncovered roasting pan, breast side up.

Immediately reduce heat to 350°. Roast for 20–25 minutes per pound or until joints pull away easily.

Baste the bird frequently with pan drippings, under and over the cloth.

Remove cloth near the end of roasting time to finish browning, and lightly salt and pepper the chicken.

## Chicken Pot Pie with Sweet Potato Crust*

*(6 servings)*

### FILLING

3 cups cooked chicken, cut in small and medium-size pieces

1 cup cooked fresh carrots, coarsely chopped

12 small, whole onions, cooked

½ cup cooked celery, minced

1 cup cooked fresh peas

1 tablespoon fresh parsley, minced

6 tablespoons chicken fat or butter (¾ stick)

6 tablespoons all-purpose flour

1 cup half-and-half

2 cups chicken broth (see Basic Chicken Broth recipe, page 89)

1 teaspoon salt

Freshly ground black pepper to taste

Preheat oven to 350°.

---

* Good recipe for leftovers

Arrange chicken, carrots, onions, celery, peas, and parsley in a 2½-quart ovenproof casserole.

In a medium-size heavy saucepan, melt chicken fat or butter over *low* heat.

Slowly stir in flour and blend until smooth.

And half-and-half and chicken broth slowly, stirring constantly.

Season with salt and freshly ground black pepper to taste.

Continue cooking and stirring until sauce is thickened.

Pour sauce over chicken and vegetables.

## SWEET POTATO CRUST

1 cup all-purpose flour, sifted

1 teaspoon baking powder

½ teaspoon salt

1 cup cold mashed sweet
  potatoes

⅓ cup lard or shortening,
  melted

1 egg, well beaten

Sprinkling flour

Sift flour together with baking powder and salt in a bowl.

Work in mashed, cold sweet potatoes with lard (or shortening) and egg.

Lightly flour a board and roll out dough with a rolling pin to about ¼ of an inch.

Cover casserole with dough and pinch edges all around.

Make a small cut in dough.

Bake pie for about 40 minutes until crust is brown.

# Baked Chicken Pancakes with Cheese Filling

2 medium-large tomatoes, peeled and coarsely chopped (with juice)

½ cup tomato juice

1 medium clove garlic, minced

1 small green pepper, minced

1 small onion, minced

½ teaspoon salt

Sprinkling of freshly ground black pepper

Pinch of oregano

1 teaspoon fresh parsley, minced

1 egg, well beaten

¼ pound cottage or ricotta cheese

1 teaspoon grated Parmesan cheese

2 large whole chicken breasts, skinned, boned, and pounded flat to about ¼ of an inch

¼ pound shredded mozzarella cheese

Preheat oven to 350°.

In a medium-size heavy saucepan combine tomatoes, tomato juice, garlic, green pepper, onion, salt, pepper, and oregano.

Place saucepan over medium heat and bring just to a boil.

Reduce heat and simmer tomato sauce for approximately 15 minutes, stirring occasionally.

Meanwhile, in a small bowl thoroughly mix parsley, well-beaten egg, cottage or ricotta cheese, and grated Parmesan cheese.

Prepare chicken breasts and cut into 8 serving pieces.

Spoon cheese mixture in the center of each piece of chicken, leaving approximately ½-inch border all around.

Roll up each piece of chicken tightly.

Spoon half the tomato sauce into a shallow baking dish large enough to hold the chicken in a single layer.

Arrange chicken rolls with the seam side down on top of tomato sauce.

Pour the remaining tomato sauce over the chicken rolls.

Sprinkle shredded mozzarella over all.

Bake for approximately 45 minutes until brown and chicken is fork-tender.

# Cap'n Charlie's
# Bits-of-Bacon Fried Chicken

2 chickens (2½–3 pounds each), cut in small serving pieces with skin intact

1 cup milk

1 egg

½ cup all-purpose flour

1 teaspoon salt

Generous sprinkling of freshly ground black pepper

Pinch of Cayenne

½ pound slab lean bacon, minced

Prepare chicken pieces and set aside.

Thoroughly beat milk with egg in a bowl or casserole dish large enough to hold chicken.

Soak chicken in milk-egg mixture and refrigerate for 1 hour.

Mix flour, salt, black pepper, and Cayenne.

Dredge chicken on all sides with flour mixture.

Spread minced bacon pieces over the bottom of a large, heavy (*cold*) skillet. *Do not cover skillet.*

Arrange chicken pieces on top of bacon in a single layer.

Fry very slowly for 45–50 minutes, until chicken is tender.

Turn carefully with tongs as chicken browns and bacon bits adhere to the pieces.

Remove chicken from the skillet with tongs and dry on absorbent paper.

Sprinkle any loose bacon pieces over chicken before serving.

## Batter-Dipped Crisp and Crunchy Fried Chicken

2 chickens (2½–3 pounds each), cut into serving pieces

2 cups water

2 bay leaves

2 whole cloves

1 medium clove garlic, minced

1 tablespoon celery seed

2 cups pancake mix

1 tablespoon salt

1 teaspoon paprika

Generous sprinkling of white pepper

2 tablespoons corn oil

2 eggs, well beaten

1⅓ cups chicken broth (see Basic Chicken Broth recipe, page 89)

2 cups corn oil

Place chicken pieces in a large kettle or Dutch oven with a tight-fitting cover.

Add water, bay leaves, cloves, garlic, and celery seed.

Cover kettle or Dutch oven and bring water to a boil.

Reduce heat and simmer for approximately 45 minutes until chicken is fork-tender.

Remove chicken and stock from heat and cool for a few minutes.

Strain and reserve 1⅓ cups of chicken stock and set aside.

Refrigerate chicken pieces for 15–20 minutes.

Thoroughly combine pancake mix, salt, paprika, white pepper, 2 tablespoons corn oil, beaten eggs, and chicken stock in a large bowl.

Generously coat each piece of chicken with the batter.

Heat 2 cups corn oil in large heavy skillet. A piece of bread dropped into the oil will turn golden brown when the temperature of the oil is just right.

Fry chicken 7–10 minutes, turning with tongs, until golden brown and crispy.

Remove chicken pieces from skillet with tongs and dry on absorbent paper.

# Monday Night Chicken Salad*

¼ cup chicken broth (see
Basic Chicken Broth recipe,
page 89)

¾ cup mayonnaise (see recipe,
page 99)

2–2½ cups cooked chicken,
cut in small pieces

1 large stalk celery, finely
chopped

1 small onion, minced

8 pimiento-stuffed olives,
finely chopped

1 small cucumber, peeled,
seeded, and finely chopped

Salt to taste

Generous sprinkling of
freshly ground black pepper

Paprika

1 tablespoon fresh parsley,
minced

Slowly blend chicken broth with mayonnaise in a small bowl. Whisk lightly and set aside.

Combine chicken, celery, onion, olives, cucumber, salt, and pepper in a medium-size bowl.

Add chicken broth and mayonnaise mixture.

Toss lightly but well.

Cover bowl and refrigerate until chilled.

Combine well before serving.

Sprinkle chicken salad with paprika and 1 tablespoon parsley before serving.

# Crispy Chicken Cutlets

2 large whole chicken breasts,
skinned, boned, and
pounded flat to about ¼ of
an inch

¼ cup mayonnaise (see recipe,
page 99)

1 cup finely crushed cornflakes

1 teaspoon salt

Sprinkling of freshly ground
black pepper

1 teaspoon vegetable oil

---

* Good recipe for leftovers

Preheat oven to 350°.

Prepare chicken breasts and cut into serving pieces.

Spread mayonnaise lightly over each side of chicken pieces.

Mix cornflakes, salt, and freshly ground black pepper.

Thoroughly coat each piece of chicken with cornflakes.

Grease a shallow baking dish (large enough to hold chicken in a single layer) with vegetable oil.

Arrange chicken cutlets in baking dish.

Bake for approximately 40 minutes until chicken is brown and crispy.

Remove cutlets to a prewarmed platter and serve immediately.

Pass Garden-Fresh Tomato Sauce (see recipe, page 105) on the side to be ladled over the chicken.

Note: A favorite chicken or brown gravy may be substituted for the tomato sauce.

# CHICKEN TIPS!

- A fresh young chicken should be pleasingly plump; moist (never slimy); have healthy-looking, undamaged skin; and no odor.

- Another method of testing if a chicken is young and fresh is to move the sharp afterend of the breastbone from side to side. If it moves easily and feels like soft rubber, take that bird home with you!

- For real economy buy chickens whole, and learn to bone and skin them as your market does. It's easier to do than you may think, and one of many available charts, pamphlets, books—or your butcher in a good mood—will help.

- Chicken should be removed from the market's plastic or paper container and wrapped loosely in waxed paper as soon as you bring it home.

- Store chicken in the coldest part of your refrigerator, and remove neck and giblets before storing.

- Always use chicken within a day or two after purchase.

- Instead of baking extra stuffing in a pan, roll stuffing into medium-size balls (approximately the size of a golf ball) and bake in a buttered muffin pan. These make interesting leftovers, topped with gravy and served with chicken or turkey.

## Mr. Lionel's Roast Wild Goose

No collection of Eastern Shore fowl recipes would be complete without including (no pun intended) one of the many ways to cook your goose. We first tasted wild goose under ideal conditions. Snow was falling heavily, and the wind was howling outside across the Chesapeake while we sat in front of a crackling fire, sipping hot buttered rum and waiting for the goose to roast. Our good friend Mr. Lionel was doing the roasting, and this is his recipe. There is none finer. The goose, when perfectly roasted, will look and taste like the finest rare roast beef you've ever had—only better.

The goose should be young and heavy for its size, with a plump and firm breast. Allow one pound of goose for each person, and a bit extra. Begin by preheating the oven to 500°.

| | |
|---|---|
| 1 quart boiling water | 1 medium stalk celery |
| 1 4½–5 pound goose, cleaned and dressed | 8–10 Maraschino cherries |
| 1 teaspoon salt | 2 tablespoons (¼ stick) butter, melted |
| Generous sprinkling of freshly ground black pepper | 3 tablespoons red cooking sherry |
| 2 large red apples, peeled, cored, and cut in quarters | |

Pour boiling water through body cavity of the goose. Thoroughly dry bird inside and out, and season with salt and pepper inside and out.

Put apples, celery, and Maraschino cherries into cavity.

Brush melted butter over skin.

Place bird on a rack in roasting pan and roast for approximately 50 minutes.

Baste goose frequently with sherry while roasting.

Remove goose from oven and discard filling.

Carve and serve immediately.

# A FINE

## OF SOUPS,

# KETTLE

# CHOWDERS, AND

# STEWS

MARYLAND WATERMEN are among the finest seafood cooks in the world, perhaps because their dishes are so plain yet inventive and their ingredients so fresh. After all, how often is it possible to put a crab, an oyster, or a fish in a pot only minutes after it's been taken from the water?

We all remember perfect moments when a certain dish tasted so very *good* because we were really hungry, and the atmosphere and the weather and all other conditions were exactly right. Such a moment for us was a crisp fall day on the Chesapeake, after a spectacular catch of rockfish (striped bass). We had been pulling them in one after another—each fish the same perfect size, as though it had been stamped from some eerie underwater mold. Our good friend Mr. Clarence put everyone to work cleaning and fillet-ing the catch, while he made his preparations for the rockfish stew recipe that follows. It's one of the no-nonsense, commonsense dishes for which Maryland watermen are famous, and we've been privileged to look over their shoulders in galleys afloat and kitchens ashore to collect some of these great recipes.

# THE RECIPES:

SMEDLEYS' LANDING WATERCRESS-CUCUMBER SOUP

OYSTER STEW MARYLAND

CREAM OF CHICKEN COOLER

SPRING ONION SOUP

ROYAL OAK CORN CHOWDER

OLD-FASHIONED CROCK SOUP

CREAM OF CRAB SOUP

CANNING HOUSE OYSTER STEW

OVEN-CLAMBAKE CHOWDER

BASIC CHICKEN BROTH

WATERMEN'S FISH CHOWDER

SCALLOPED TOMATO SOUP

MR. CLARENCE'S ROCKFISH STEW

RALPH'S ONE-TWO CRAB SOUP

FARMERS' CHICKEN-VEGETABLE CHOWDER

WINTER CABBAGE SOUP

# Smedleys' Landing Watercress-Cucumber Soup

4 cups chicken broth (see Basic Chicken Broth recipe, page 89)

1 small bunch watercress, coarsely chopped

1 medium onion, coarsely chopped

1 medium cucumber, peeled, seeded, and coarsely chopped

Generous sprinkling of freshly ground black pepper

Salt to taste

Pinch dry mustard (optional)

Bring chicken broth to a boil in a medium-size heavy saucepan.

Reduce heat immediately and add watercress, onion, and cucumber.

Sprinkle generously with freshly ground black pepper.

Simmer for 12–15 minutes until vegetables "wilt."

Add salt to taste.

A pinch of dry mustard may be stirred into the soup just before serving.

# Oyster Stew Maryland

4 tablespoons (½ stick) butter

½ cup cooked minced celery

1 pint freshly shucked oysters with liquor

1 cup half-and-half

3 cups milk

Dash of salt

* Paprika (optional)

Melt butter in the top part of a double boiler over boiling water, and lightly sauté celery. The pan should be *over* and not *in* the water.

Add oysters with liquor, half-and-half, milk, and salt.

Cook slowly until the edges of the oysters just begin to curl and the half-and-half/milk mixture is hot. (The oysters will float.)

Sprinkle stew lightly with paprika* and serve immediately.

─────────

* Seafood seasoning may be substituted for paprika.

# Cream of Chicken Cooler

*(6–8 servings)*

5 cups chicken broth (see Basic Chicken Broth recipe, page 89)

4 egg yolks

2 cups warm heavy cream

2 teaspoons curry powder

Dash of Cayenne

Salt to taste

Sprinkling of white pepper

Few drops of fresh lemon juice

1 cup cooked, chilled white meat chicken, finely chopped

1 tablespoon fresh parsley, minced

Heat chicken broth to scalding in the top part of a double boiler.

Separate eggs, putting yolks in a small bowl and setting whites aside for another use.

Thoroughly combine yolks, cream, curry powder, and Cayenne, whisking all together for a few seconds.

Stir 2 tablespoons of hot chicken broth into the yolks and cream.

Mix well and blend yolks and cream mixture into the chicken broth in the top part of the double boiler, reducing heat. Cook, stirring constantly, until it just begins to thicken.

Remove from heat and set aside to cool.

Season with salt, white pepper, and lemon juice.

When soup is cool, cover and refrigerate until thoroughly chilled.

Stir in chicken meat before serving, and sprinkle with parsley.

Note: Chilled bowls make the soup seem even cooler on a hot summer day.

## Spring Onion Soup

1 bunch green onions
(scallions) with tops, cut in
1-inch pieces

3 cups chicken broth (see
Basic Chicken Broth recipe,
page 89)

3 tablespoons butter, softened

1 tablespoon all-purpose flour

Sprinkling of white pepper

1 cup half-and-half

½ cup light cream

Salt to taste

Simmer scallions in chicken broth in a medium-size heavy saucepan until soft, about 15 minutes.

Thoroughly blend softened butter with flour, white pepper, half-and-half, and cream in a small bowl.

Stir batter mixture into saucepan with scallions and broth.

Heat soup just to boiling, stirring slowly with a wooden spoon.

Salt to taste before serving.

## Royal Oak Corn Chowder

4 large ears of fresh young
corn, kernels cut from the
cob

2 cups milk

2 cups half-and-half

2 egg yolks

2 tablespoons (¼ stick) butter,
softened

1 teaspoon salt

1 teaspoon sugar

Sprinkling of white pepper

Paprika

Place corn, milk, and half-and-half in a medium-size heavy saucepan over low heat.

Separate eggs, putting yolks in a small bowl and setting whites aside for another use.

Whisk softened butter into egg yolks.

Add 1 tablespoon of warm corn-milk mixture to the egg yolks and butter.

Whisk again to mix well.

Stir mixture into the saucepan with corn and milk.

Add salt, sugar, and white pepper.

Heat chowder just to boiling, stirring slowly with a wooden spoon.

Sprinkle with paprika before serving.


## Old-Fashioned Crock Soup*

*(8 servings)*

6 medium-large potatoes, peeled and sliced

1 large onion, cut in 8 slices

6 medium tomatoes, cut in half

1 small yellow turnip, peeled and coarsely chopped

2½ cups fresh, shelled green peas

1 medium carrot, finely chopped

¼ cup raw rice

1 tablespoon salt

1 tablespoon sugar

Generous sprinkling of freshly ground black pepper

Pinch of ground allspice

2 quarts chicken broth (see Basic Chicken Broth recipe, page 89)

Preheat oven to 300°.

Arrange vegetables and rice in alternate layers in a Dutch oven, large bean pot, or a stone crock (if you're lucky enough to have one!) that has a tight-fitting cover. A large casserole dish may also be used.

Add seasonings.

Pour 2 quarts of broth over vegetables.

Cover tightly, using tape if the lid alone is not tight enough.

Set pot or casserole in the oven in a pan of hot water.

Cook for 6 hours and serve immediately.

———————

* Six-hour recipe

## Cream of Crab Soup

2 tablespoons (¼ stick) butter

1 small onion, minced

1 pound backfin crabmeat

2 egg yolks

Sprinkling of white pepper

Salt to taste

Pinch of paprika

Pinch of Cayenne

Dash of Worcestershire sauce

2 cups warm milk

1½ cups warm half-and-half

1 tablespoon fresh parsley, minced

Melt butter in the top part of a double boiler over boiling water.

Stir in onion and sauté until soft.

Add crabmeat.

Separate eggs, putting yolks in a small bowl and setting whites aside for another use.

Whisk yolks briskly with pepper, salt, paprika, Cayenne, and Worcestershire sauce. Blend this mixture with the crabmeat.

Slowly add milk and half-and-half, stirring constantly.

Reduce heat under double boiler.

Cook soup slowly for about 15 minutes, stirring occasionally with a wooden spoon.

Sprinkle with parsley before serving.


## Canning House Oyster Stew

8 tablespoons (1 stick) butter

1 pint shucked oysters, with liquor

Dash of Worcestershire sauce

Pinch of Cayenne pepper

4 cups warm milk ⎫ or 8 cups
4 cups light cream ⎭ half-&-half

1 teaspoon salt

Sprinkling of white pepper

4 tablespoons (½ stick) butter

Paprika

Melt butter in a large heavy saucepan over low heat.

Add oysters with liquor, Worcestershire, and Cayenne.

Simmer until edges of oysters just begin to curl.

Slowly stir in warm milk and cream (or half-and-half).

Season with salt and white pepper.

Heat slowly until hot, being careful not to let oyster stew come to a boil.

Ladle stew into 4 soup bowls.

Top each serving with 1 tablespoon of butter.

Sprinkle with paprika and serve immediately.


## Oven-Clambake Chowder

¼ pound salt pork, minced

3 large potatoes, coarsely chopped

1 medium-large onion, finely chopped

2–4 ears of fresh corn (to make about 1½–2 cups), freshly cut from the cob

2 dozen shucked soft-shell clams with liquor, coarsely chopped

1 cup crushed soda crackers

1 teaspoon salt

Sprinkling of freshly ground black pepper

2–3 cups milk

1 cup crushed soda crackers

Paprika

Preheat oven to 350°.

Arrange salt pork, potatoes, onion, corn, clams with liquor, and 1 cup of crushed soda crackers in alternate layers in an ovenproof casserole.

Season with salt and pepper.

Pour milk over all. Add more milk if necessary, so that liquid is approximately 1 inch above the vegetables.

Sprinkle 1 cup crushed soda crackers over top of casserole.

Dust with paprika.

Bake chowder for approximately 1 hour until potatoes are tender and most of the liquid has been absorbed.

# Basic Chicken Broth

*(about 1 quart)*

1 stewing chicken (3–3½ pounds), cut in small pieces

2 quarts cold water

1 medium-large onion, sliced

1 medium-large carrot, coarsely chopped

1 bay leaf

1 teaspoon salt

2–3 sprigs parsley

Cut chicken in small pieces and crack bones.

Place chicken pieces in a large kettle.

Add 2 quarts cold water and let stand for 30 minutes.

Bring water to a boil and add all other ingredients.

Reduce heat and cover kettle. Simmer chicken and broth, covered, for 3 hours.

Remove kettle from heat and strain broth. Set broth aside to cool.

When broth is cool, skim off any fat from the top.

Refrigerate broth in a closed container until ready to use.

Remove chicken from bones and set aside for another use.

# Watermen's Fish Chowder

*(4–6 servings)*

1 pound rockfish (striped bass) fillets, cut in serving pieces

1 bay leaf

1 cup cold water

2 tablespoons (¼ stick) butter

1 medium-large onion, finely chopped

2 medium-large potatoes, peeled and diced

1 large stalk celery, minced

1 cup cold water

2 cups warm milk

1 cup warm light cream

Salt to taste

White or freshly ground black pepper to taste

Pats of butter

Paprika

Place rockfish fillets in a large, heavy kettle or saucepan with bay leaf and 1 cup of cold water.

Simmer over low heat until fish flakes easily with a fork.

Remove fish from the kettle/saucepan with a slotted spoon, and set aside.

Discard bay leaf.

Pour off fish stock and set aside.

Melt butter in the kettle/saucepan and sauté onion until soft.

Add potatoes, celery, and 1 cup of cold water.

Cover kettle/saucepan and cook vegetables over medium heat for approximately 10 minutes until potatoes and celery are tender.

Slowly stir in milk and light cream.

Flake fish and return it to the kettle with the fish stock.

Heat chowder just to boiling, stirring slowly with a wooden spoon.

Season with salt and pepper.

Before serving, top each portion with a pat of butter and sprinkle lightly with paprika.


## Scalloped Tomato Soup

**1 medium-large onion, finely chopped**

**2 tablespoons (¼ stick) butter**

**2 large tomatoes, peeled and finely chopped**

**1 teaspoon salt**

**4 whole black peppercorns**

**1 teaspoon light brown sugar**

**1 bay leaf**

**2–3 sprigs fresh parsley, minced**

**4 cups chicken broth (see Basic Chicken Broth recipe, page 89)**

**3 slices white bread with crust, cut in cubes about ½ of an inch**

**2 tablespoons (¼ stick) butter**

Sauté onions in butter in a large heavy saucepan until soft.

Stir in tomatoes, salt, peppercorns, brown sugar, bay leaf, and parsley.

Simmer for approximately 5 minutes.

Add chicken broth and cover saucepan. Cook over low heat for about 15 minutes.

Fry bread cubes in butter in a medium-size skillet, turning them with tongs until brown and crisp.

Place bread cubes in each soup bowl.

Ladle soup over bread and serve immediately.

## Mr. Clarence's Rockfish Stew

1½–2 pounds rockfish (striped bass) fillets, cut in serving pieces

6 thick slices bacon

½ cup all-purpose flour

½ teaspoon salt

Sprinkling of white pepper

½ cup half-and-half or light cream

4–5 medium potatoes, peeled and sliced about ¼ of an inch thick

1 small bunch green onions (scallions) with tops, cut in 1-inch pieces

2–2½ cups cold water

Prepare rockfish fillets and set aside.

Sauté bacon in a large, heavy skillet until crisp.

Remove bacon from skillet with a slotted spoon and set aside.

Mix flour, salt, and white pepper.

Dip fish fillets in cream and then coat on both sides with seasoned flour.

Sauté in bacon drippings approximately 2 minutes on each side until fish is golden brown. Turn carefully with tongs.

Place potato slices over the fish fillets.

Sprinkle green onion pieces over the potatoes.

Add water.

Cover skillet and simmer for approximately 20 minutes, or until potatoes are tender.

Crumble bacon pieces over all before serving.

Note: A little flour mixed with water may be added to the skillet if you prefer a thicker stew.

# Ralph's One-Two Crab Soup

*(6 servings)*

2 ounces salt pork or slab bacon (rind removed), finely chopped

1 large onion, coarsely chopped

1 large carrot, coarsely chopped

1 large stalk celery, coarsely chopped

2 medium-large tomatoes, peeled and coarsely chopped

1 large or 2 medium potatoes, peeled and coarsely chopped

1 teaspoon seafood seasoning or to taste

1 teaspoon Worcestershire sauce

1 quart cold water

1 pound backfin crabmeat

Salt to taste

Freshly ground black pepper to taste

Sauté salt pork/bacon in small, heavy skillet until golden brown and crispy. Remove from skillet with a slotted spoon and set aside. Reserve fat for another use.

Place all vegetables, seafood seasoning, and Worcestershire sauce in a large heavy kettle or Dutch oven.

Pour water over all and bring to a boil.

Reduce heat and simmer for 25–30 minutes until vegetables are tender.

Stir in crabmeat and mix well.

Sprinkle salt pork/bacon over all.

Simmer for 2 or 3 more minutes.

# Farmers' Chicken-Vegetable Chowder

*(6 servings)*

1 medium-large onion, finely chopped

1 small green pepper, finely chopped

1 small sweet red pepper, finely chopped

3 large ripe tomatoes, peeled and coarsely chopped

1 medium zucchini, diced

1 small yellow squash, cut in thin strips

2 medium carrots, thinly sliced

1 large stalk celery (with leaves), sliced

½ pound small, whole green beans, ends snapped off

2 small white turnips, peeled and thinly sliced

5 cups chicken broth (see Basic Chicken Broth recipe, page 89)

⅓ cup raw rice

1–1½ cups cooked chicken, cut in small pieces

2 green onions (scallions), with tops, cut in 1-inch pieces

Place all vegetables, except scallions, with chicken broth in a large heavy kettle or Dutch oven.

Bring broth to a boil.

Reduce heat and simmer for approximately 10 minutes.

Stir in rice.

Cover kettle or Dutch oven and simmer broth and vegetables for 15–20 minutes, until rice is cooked.

Add chicken and green onions and mix well.

Simmer for 2 or 3 more minutes.

Season individually with salt and freshly ground black pepper.

# Winter Cabbage Soup

*(4–6 servings)*

1 soup bone (about 1½–
   2 pounds)

1 quart cold water

1 teaspoon salt

Sprinkling of white pepper

1 bay leaf

1 medium-large head cabbage,
   cored and coarsely chopped

2 tablespoons (¼ stick) butter

1 medium-large onion,
   coarsely chopped

2 tablespoons (¼ stick) butter

1 medium-large stalk celery
   (with leaves), finely
   chopped

1 bunch young, fresh beet
   greens (tops) with stems,
   coarsely chopped

½ cup heavy cream

Salt to taste

Put soup bone with water, salt, pepper, and bay leaf in a large heavy kettle or Dutch oven.

Bring water to a boil.

Reduce heat and simmer, covered, for 2 hours.

Brown cabbage quickly in butter in a large heavy skillet, for 2–3 minutes.

Remove cabbage from skillet/Dutch oven with a slotted spoon and add to the soup stock.

In the skillet, sauté onion in butter until golden. Remove onion and add to the stock with celery and beet greens.

Continue cooking soup over low heat for approximately 1 hour.

Remove soup bone.

Whip cream with salt in a small bowl.

Serve soup piping hot with a dollop of salted whipped cream on top.

# SOUP TIPS!

- A light soup, either chilled or piping hot, is a pleasant and surprising change from your usual breakfast fare.

- Chilled soups, first served in England by French gourmets in the eighteenth century, soon turned up on Maryland tables. Always serve chilled soups *icy* cold, being sure to allow enough time in the refrigerator to chill them properly.

- Place a lettuce leaf on hot soup to remove any grease. Discard the lettuce just before serving soup.

- Always make more soup than you think you'll need. Most soups taste as good or even better the second day.

- Lightly grease the bottom of a saucepan when heating milk to prevent it from scorching or sticking.

- Place a slice of raw potato in soup that has been oversalted. Cook with soup for approximately 10 minutes, and remove the potato while it is still crisp.

- Toast bite-size cereals in a 300° oven for approximately 15 minutes, and use intead of croutons.

# DOWN-HOME

# SAUCES,

# RELISHES,
# AND DRESSINGS

## THE RECIPES:

## Salisbury
## Tomato-Pepper Relish

*(about 2 cups)*

2 large ripe tomatoes or 3–4 medium-size tomatoes, peeled and diced (about ½ inch)

1 small green pepper, minced

1 medium stalk celery, finely chopped

1 small onion, minced

1 small carrot, minced

1 teaspoon salt

Generous sprinkling of freshly ground black pepper

2 tablespoons sugar

2 tablespoons cider vinegar

½ cup cold water

Prepare tomatoes and put them in a medium-size bowl with all other ingredients.

Lightly toss, cover, and refrigerate relish for 3–4 hours.

Drain before serving.

## Taylors Island
## Tartar Sauce

*(about 1¼ cups)*

1 cup basic mayonnaise (see recipe, page 99)

1 hard-cooked egg, finely chopped

1 teaspoon fresh parsley, minced

1 small dill pickle (about 1 tablespoon), minced and drained

Salt to taste

Sprinkling of white pepper (optional)

2–3 pimiento-stuffed olives, minced

Thoroughly combine all ingredients and chill for at least 2 hours before serving.

Note: Sauce may be thinned with a few drops of lemon juice if it becomes too thick.

## Homemade Mayonnaise

*(about 1½ cups)*

**2 egg yolks**
**1 tablespoon wine vinegar**
**½ teaspoon salt**

**¼ teaspoon dry mustard**
**½ cup olive oil**
**½ cup peanut oil**

Remove eggs from refrigerator and let stand for 2 hours.

Separate eggs, putting yolks in a small bowl and setting whites aside for another use.

Whisk yolks briskly until they begin to get thick and creamy.

Add vinegar, salt, and mustard.

Continue whisking for about 1 minute until well blended.

*Slowly* add the olive oil a drop at a time, whisking briskly and constantly. If oil is added too quickly the mayonnaise will curdle.

Add the peanut oil the same way, *slowly*, whisking briskly to be sure all oil is being absorbed by the eggs.

Add a few drops more vinegar if mayonnaise is too thick.

Note: If mayonnaise separates while being stored in the refrigerator, you can bring it back by slowly beating an egg yolk into the mixture.

# Summer-Cooler
# Salad Dressing

*(about 1½ cups)*

1 cup sour cream

1 small cucumber, peeled, seeded, and finely chopped

1 green onion (scallion) with tops, thinly sliced

4 radishes, finely chopped

1 small green pepper, minced

1 tablespoon tarragon vinegar

1 tablespoon prepared horseradish, or to taste

Salt to taste

1 teaspoon half-and-half

Combine all ingredients, cover, and refrigerate.

Thoroughly mix before serving.


# Grandma Mame's
# Fruit Salad Dressing

*(about 1½ cups)*

¾ cup basic mayonnaise (see recipe, page 99)

¼ cup heavy cream, whipped

¼ cup salted almonds, finely chopped

¼ cup apple, grape, or currant (or other favorite) jelly

Combine mayonnaise and whipped cream in a small bowl.

Stir in chopped almonds.

Add favorite flavor jelly.

Whisk all ingredients briskly until well blended, for approximately 1 minute.

Cover and refrigerate until ready to use.

Whisk briskly again before serving.

## Company's Comin' Salad Dressing

*(about 2 cups)*

½ cup cider vinegar

1½ cups olive oil (or other salad oil)

2–3 cloves garlic, minced

2 teaspoons salt

Generous sprinkling of freshly ground black pepper

1 small onion, minced

1 teaspoon dry mustard

Pinch of Cayenne

⅓ cup chili sauce

1 tablespoon prepared horseradish

1 teaspoon paprika

1 tablespoon fresh parsley, minced

Put all ingredients in a 1-quart glass jar with a tight-fitting lid.

Shake vigorously until well blended, and refrigerate.

Note: Thoroughly shake the dressing each time before using.

## Whipped Cream Dressing for Potato Salad

*(about 2 cups)*

1 cup basic mayonnaise (see recipe, page 99)

½ cup heavy cream, whipped

½ cup sour cream

2 hard-cooked eggs, finely chopped

1 tablespoon fresh chives, minced

Salt to taste

Generous sprinkling of white pepper

Mix all ingredients in a medium-size bowl.

Whisk lightly but well for about 1 minute before combining with potato salad.

## Cambridge-Style
## Corn Relish

*(about 4 cups)*

6–8 ears of fresh corn (to make about 4 cups), kernels cut from cob

1 large onion, finely chopped

1 medium-size sweet red pepper, finely chopped

1 medium green pepper, finely chopped

2 large stalks celery, finely chopped

1 teaspoon dry mustard

¼ cup dark brown sugar

1 tablespoon salt

Generous sprinkling of freshly ground black pepper

¾ cup cider vinegar

Combine all ingredients in a large heavy saucepan.

Bring mixture to a boil. Reduce heat and simmer for 15–20 minutes. Then set aside to cool.

Refrigerate corn relish in a covered glass dish or bowl.

Mix well before serving.

Note: Relish should be used within 24 hours for best taste.

## Chilled
## Mustard-Relish Sauce

*(about ½ cup)*

1 tablespoon corn oil

2 tablespoons cider vinegar

1 small onion, minced

1 tablespoon Dijon (or other mild) mustard

1 teaspoon sugar

2 hard-cooked egg yolks, finely chopped

1 small sweet pickle, minced and drained

1 tablespoon heavy cream

Whisk corn oil and vinegar together in a small bowl.

Add all other ingredients and blend well.

Cover bowl and refrigerate until chilled.

Mix well before serving.

## Chilled-and-Spicy Tomato Sauce

*(about 1 cup)*

¾ cup chili sauce

Prepared horseradish to taste

1 teaspoon Worcestershire
   sauce

1 small lemon (juice)

Dash of Tabasco sauce

1 medium clove garlic, minced

1 small onion, minced

1 small stalk celery, minced

Salt to taste

Generous sprinkling of
   freshly ground black pepper

Combine all ingredients and mix thoroughly.

Refrigerate in a tightly covered container until ready to use.

Mix well before serving.

## The Devil's Butter

*(about ¾ cup)*

8 tablespoons (1 stick) sweet
   butter, softened

1 small clove garlic, minced

½ teaspoon dry mustard

2 teaspoons wine vinegar

Generous dash of
   Worcestershire sauce

Dash of Tabasco sauce

Salt to taste

Pinch of Cayenne

1 teaspoon fresh parsley,
   minced

2 egg yolks

Soften butter in a small bowl and thoroughly combine all other ingredients except egg yolks.

Separate eggs, putting yolks in another small bowl and setting whites aside for another use.

Whisk yolks briskly until they begin to get thick and creamy.

Add yolks to butter and continue whisking until well blended.

Note: This butter should be used within 24 hours for best taste.

## Old-Fashioned Boiled Salad Dressing

*(about 2½ cups)*

¼ cup sugar

1 teaspoon salt

2 tablespoons all-purpose flour

1 tablespoon dry mustard

Dash of paprika

4 egg yolks, well beaten

4 tablespoons (½ stick) butter, melted

1½ cups milk

⅓ cup cider vinegar

Combine sugar, salt, flour, mustard, and paprika in the top part of a double boiler.

Separate eggs, putting yolks in a small bowl and setting whites aside for another use.

Whisk yolks briskly until they begin to get thick and creamy.

Add egg yolks, melted butter, and milk to the dry ingredients and mix thoroughly.

Place top part of double boiler over boiling water.

Slowly add vinegar and cook mixture, stirring constantly, until it thickens.

Remove from heat and chill.

Note: This is a tasty dressing to be tossed with coleslaw or cold diced potatoes.

# Apple-Turnip Relish*

*(about 3 cups)*

2 young, medium-size yellow turnips (to make about 2½ cups), peeled and finely chopped

1 medium onion, finely chopped

1 large, ripe, red apple, peeled, cored and finely chopped

¼ cup light brown sugar

¼ cup cider vinegar

2 tablespoons corn oil

2 teaspoons cold water

½ teaspoon salt

Generous sprinkling of white pepper

Combine all ingredients in a medium-size bowl and toss lightly but well.

Cover bowl and refrigerate overnight.

Mix well before serving.

Note: Relish should be used within 48 hours for best taste.

# Garden-Fresh Tomato Sauce

*(about 2 cups)*

1 large clove garlic, minced

1 large onion, coarsely chopped

1 tablespoon corn oil

1 medium-large green pepper, coarsely chopped

1 medium stalk celery, thinly sliced

1 teaspoon salt

Generous sprinkling of freshly ground black pepper

3 large ripe tomatoes, peeled and coarsely chopped (with juice)

---

* Overnight recipe

Sauté garlic and onion in oil in a medium-size, heavy skillet until onion is soft.

Add green pepper, celery, salt, and black pepper to the skillet.

Reduce heat and continue cooking and stirring vegetables slowly for about 3 minutes.

Thoroughly mix tomatoes and their juice with the vegetables.

Simmer for 30–35 minutes, stirring often until sauce is thickened. If you prefer a thinner sauce, add a little tomato juice.

Serve piping hot!

## Velvet Cream Sauce for Chicken

*(about 2 cups)*

2 cups chicken broth (see Basic Chicken Broth recipe, page 89)

1 medium onion, finely chopped

1 large stalk celery, finely chopped

1 bay leaf

2 sprigs fresh parsley

1 small carrot, finely chopped

2 tablespoons (¼ stick) butter

2 tablespoons all-purpose flour

½ cup light cream

Salt to taste

Generous sprinkling of freshly ground black pepper

Paprika

Simmer chicken broth with onion, celery, bay leaf, parsley, and carrot in a small, heavy saucepan for 30 minutes.

Strain broth and set aside.

In a medium-size, heavy saucepan stir butter and flour together over low heat for approximately 5 minutes, until well blended.

Slowly add cream and chicken broth, and continue cooking and stirring constantly over low heat until sauce is thickened. Add a bit more broth if sauce becomes too thick.

Season with salt and pepper.

Continue cooking over low heat for approximately 10 minutes, stirring constantly.

Serve immediately, sprinkled with paprika.

# VEGETABLES

# FROM THE GARDEN

## THE RECIPES:

*A*

ASPARAGUS SPEARS (WITH THE DEVIL'S BUTTER)
ASPARAGUS SOUFFLÉ
ASPARAGUS CRUMBLE

*B*

SAVORY SKILLET GREEN BEANS
MISS MINNIE'S CHILLED-AND-TANGY
  GREEN BEAN STRIPS
PUFFED GREEN BEAN CASSEROLE

SPICY LIMA BEAN BAKE
LIMAS, APPLES, 'N ONIONS
LIMA BEANS AU GRATIN

BUTTERED BEETS AND GREENS
CRISPY BAKED BEET CASSEROLE

AUNT SALLIE'S SATURDAY-NIGHT BAKED BEANS

BROCCOLI HEAD WITH LEMON BUTTER
BROCCOLI SALAD APPETIZER

HOME-FRIED BRUSSELS SPROUTS
BRUSSELLS SPROUTS GARDEN SPECIAL

## C

WATERMEN'S CABBAGE
CHURCH CREEK CABBAGE WITH TART SAUCE
SUNDAY'S COUNTRY SLAW

CREAMY MASHED CARROTS
JACK'S CARROT BURGERS

CAULIFLOWER HEAD WITH EGG SAUCE
COUNTRIFRIED CAULIFLOWER

WYE MILLS CELERY CASSEROLE

SOUTHERN-FRIED CORN
COUNTRY -STYLE CREAMED CORN

HOOPERS ISLAND FRIED CUCUMBERS

## E

DOSSIE'S ELEGANT PICNIC EGGPLANT

## G

GARDEN-FRESH GREENS:
  BEET TOPS
  COLLARDS
  DANDELIONS
  KALE
  MUSTARD
  SPINACH
  SWISS CHARD
  TURNIPS

*O*

OTTIE'S OKRA

*P*

TILGHMAN HASH-BROWN PARSNIPS

PEAS IN BLANKETS

COUNTRY POTATO SALAD
TART-AND-SWEET SKILLET POTATOES
MAPLE-CANDIED SWEET POTATOES

ROASTED PUMPKIN SEEDS SNACK

*S*

BAKED STUFFED WINTER SQUASH
SUMMER SQUASH CASSEROLE (ZUCCHINI)

*T*

TRAPPE GREEN TOMATO FRY
OLD-FASHIONED SCALLOPED TOMATOES

MARY ELLEN'S BUTTERY MASHED TURNIPS

# Asparagus Spears

*(with The Devil's Butter)*

| | |
|---|---|
| **2 pounds fresh asparagus spears** | **Water to cover** |
| **1 teaspoon salt** | |

Clean and wash asparagus thoroughly. Scrape the spears carefully starting about 2 inches from the top of each spear. Trim off any tough ends.

In a large heavy skillet bring enough salted water to a boil to cover the asparagus in a single layer.

Add asparagus and simmer from 3–5 minutes, or until spears are tender-crisp.

Drain immediately and arrange spears on a preheated platter.

Top with pats of The Devil's Butter (see recipe, page 103) to serve.

Note: Asparagus spears may also be tied with white string and cooked upright in a coffee pot. Add spears to ½ cup of boiling salted water. Cover coffee pot tightly and simmer asparagus for 8–10 minutes, or until spears are tender-crisp.

# Asparagus Soufflé

| | |
|---|---|
| **3 tablespoons butter, melted** | **1–1½ pounds cooked, fresh asparagus spears, cut in 1-inch pieces** |
| **3 tablespoons all-purpose flour** | |
| **1 cup milk** | **½ teaspoon salt** |
| **4 eggs, separated** | **Sprinkling of white pepper** |

Preheat oven to 325°.

Blend butter into flour in a medium-size heavy saucepan over low heat.

Slowly add milk, stirring constantly with a wooden spoon until sauce begins to thicken.

Separate eggs, putting yolks in a small bowl and setting whites aside for later use.

Whisk yolks briskly until they begin to get thick and creamy.

Combine asparagus, salt, and white pepper with the yolks, transfer to a saucepan, and mix gently but well.

Whisk egg whites in a small bowl until stiff.

Fold egg whites carefully into the asparagus mixture and pour all into a lightly greased, ovenproof casserole.

Set casserole in a pan of hot water and bake for approximately 45 minutes, until soufflé is set.

## *Asparagus Crumble*

**2 pounds cooked fresh asparagus spears**

**1 cup dry bread crumbs**

**1 egg, well beaten**

**1 teaspoon milk**

**Dash of salt**

**Sprinkling of freshly ground black pepper**

**8 tablespoons (1 stick) butter**

Roll asparagus spears in bread crumbs.

Whisk egg and milk together in a small, flat dish.

Dip spears into egg and milk mixture and roll again in crumbs.

Sprinkle with salt and pepper.

Heat butter in a large heavy skillet until just sizzling.

Brown asparagus spears quickly in butter, turning with tongs.

Arrange on a preheated platter and serve immediately.

Drizzle any remaining butter over top of spears with crumbs from the skillet.

# Savory Skillet Green Beans

1 pound young, whole green beans, ends snapped off

1 cup cold water

½ teaspoon salt

3 thick slices bacon

1 medium onion, finely chopped

1 small stalk celery, finely chopped

1 large clove garlic, minced

2–3 sprigs fresh parsley, minced

1 large pimiento, drained and coarsely chopped

Salt to taste

Freshly ground black pepper to taste

Wash and trim beans.

Bring water and salt to a boil in a medium-size, heavy saucepan.

Add beans, cover, and cook for approximately 15 minutes until beans are tender-crisp.

Drain beans, and set them aside, keeping them warm.

Sauté bacon in a large, heavy skillet until crisp.

Remove bacon from skillet with a slotted spoon and set aside.

Sauté onion, celery, garlic, and parsley in bacon fat until soft.

Add beans to skillet and top with pimiento.

Season with salt and pepper to taste.

Toss beans lightly but well and cover.

Cook over low heat for approximately 5 minutes.

Crumble bacon pieces over beans before serving.

# Miss Minnie's Chilled-and-Tangy Green Bean Strips

⅓ cup corn oil

¼ cup cider vinegar

1 small onion, minced

Dash Worcestershire sauce

1 small clove garlic, minced

1 small green pepper, minced

½ teaspoon salt

Generous sprinkling of freshly ground black pepper

1 pound cooked, young green beans, each cut lengthwise in 2 or 3 strips

4 hard-cooked eggs, finely chopped

¼ cup mayonnaise (see recipe, page 99)

1 small pimiento, drained and finely chopped

1 teaspoon prepared mustard

4 large lettuce leaves

Whisk oil, vinegar, onion, Worcestershire sauce, garlic, green pepper, and salt and pepper together in a small bowl.

Place green bean strips in a wide salad bowl.

Pour oil and vinegar mixture over the beans.

Cover salad bowl and refrigerate until thoroughly chilled.

Thoroughly mix eggs, mayonnaise, pimiento, and mustard in a small bowl.

Combine with chilled green beans and dressing.

Toss lightly until well blended.

Serve bean strips mixture on lettuce leaves.

# Puffed Green Bean Casserole

1 pound small, young, whole green beans, ends snapped off and cooked

1 medium stalk celery (with leaves), finely chopped

¾ cup mayonnaise (see recipe, page 99)

¼ teaspoon dry mustard

¼ teaspoon salt

Sprinkling of white pepper

1 teaspoon cider vinegar

¼ cup milk

1 egg white

Paprika

Preheat oven to 400°.

Place whole, cooked green beans in an ovenproof casserole.

Sprinkle celery over beans.

Blend mayonnaise, mustard, salt, white pepper, and vinegar in a small bowl.

Gradually mix in milk.

Separate egg, putting the white in a small bowl and setting the yolk aside for another use.

Whisk egg white until stiff.

Fold egg white carefully into mayonnaise mixture and pile on top of green beans.

Dust top with paprika.

Bake for approximately 15 minutes until sauce puffs up and browns and beans are heated through.


## Spicy Lima Bean Bake

2 cups cooked fresh lima beans

¼ pound slab bacon (rind removed), finely chopped

1 large onion, finely chopped

1 small green pepper, finely chopped

1 medium clove garlic, minced

2 medium-large tomatoes, peeled and finely chopped (with juice)

1 tablespoon molasses

1 tablespoon dark brown sugar

1 teaspoon salt

Generous sprinkling of freshly ground black pepper

Pinch of dry mustard

Pinch of Cayenne

Preheat oven to 300°.

Thoroughly combine all ingredients in a lightly greased, ovenproof casserole.

Bake for approximately 1 hour.

# Limas, Apples, 'n Onions

1 large red onion, finely
   chopped

3 tablespoons butter

¼ teaspoon turmeric

½ teaspoon ground allspice

Sprinkling of freshly ground
   black pepper

1 teaspoon salt

1 large tart apple, peeled,
   cored, and coarsely chopped

2 cups cooked, fresh lima
   beans

½ cup chicken broth (see
   Basic Chicken Broth recipe,
   page 89)

Sauté onion in butter in a large heavy skillet until soft.

Stir in turmeric, allspice, pepper, and salt.

Add apple and continue cooking over low heat, stirring constantly until apple begins to soften.

Mix in lima beans and chicken broth.

Cover skillet and simmer mixture for 8–10 minutes.

Pour in a little more chicken broth if lima beans seem too dry.

# Lima Beans au Gratin

2 cups cooked fresh lima
   beans

2 tablespoons butter

2 tablespoons all-purpose
   flour

1 teaspoon salt

Sprinkling of white pepper

Dash Worcestershire sauce

Pinch of Cayenne

1 cup light cream

½ cup grated Parmesan cheese

2 tablespoons butter

Preheat oven to 375°.

Place lima beans in a shallow ovenproof casserole.

Melt 2 tablespoons of butter in a small heavy saucepan.

Mix in flour, salt, white pepper, Worcestershire sauce, and Cayenne.

Slowly stir in cream and cook over low heat, stirring constantly, until sauce begins to thicken.

Pour sauce over lima beans.

Sprinkle grated Parmesan over top of casserole.

Dot with remaining 2 tablespoons of butter.

Bake for approximately 25 minutes, until heated through and grated cheese is nicely browned.


## Buttered Beets and Greens

| | |
|---|---|
| **2 pounds young small or medium-size beets with tops** | **8 tablespoons (1 stick) butter, melted** |
| **Boiling water** | **Salt to taste** |
| **½ teaspoon salt** | **Freshly ground black pepper to taste** |
| **Green beet tops** | |

Leave roots on beets and cut off green tops, leaving about 2 inches of the stems.

Set green tops aside for later use.

Wash beets carefully (do not scrub), without breaking skin or roots.

Cover beats with boiling water in a medium-size saucepan.

Cover saucepan and cook beets until tender, approximately 30 minutes to 1 hour, depending on their size.

Drain beets and cool quickly under cold water.

Drain again, and slip skins gently off beets.

Cut off stems and set aside to be added to green tops.

Discard roots.

If beets are small, leave whole.

Cut in quarters if beets are medium-size.

Thoroughly wash beet tops in lukewarm water and discard any wilted leaves.

Rinse several times in cold water to remove all sand.

Place beet tops in a medium-size, heavy saucepan.

Do not add water and cover tightly.

Cook greens over low heat for 10–15 minutes.

Drain.

Add beets to beet tops and toss lightly with butter.

Season to taste with salt and pepper before serving.


## Crispy Baked Beet Casserole

4 tablespoons (½ stick) butter, melted

4 tablespoons all-purpose flour

1 cup cold water

3 tablespoons dark brown sugar

Pinch of salt

2 tablespoons horseradish

2 pounds cooked beets (see Buttered Beets and Greens recipe, page 118) cut in half

⅓ cup dry bread crumbs

3 tablespoons butter

Preheat oven to 375°.

Thoroughly blend melted butter with flour over low heat.

Gradually mix in water, stirring constantly, until sauce begins to thicken.

Add brown sugar, salt, horseradish, and beets.

Mix lightly but well.

Pour beets and sauce into a lightly greased baking dish.

Sprinkle bread crumbs over top and dot with butter.

Bake for 20–25 minutes until crumbs are nicely browned.

# Aunt Sallie's Saturday Night Baked Beans*

*(4–6 servings)*

| | |
|---|---|
| 1 pound dry pea beans | 1 teaspoon dry mustard |
| ¾ slab of fat salt pork, cut in half | ¼ cup dark brown sugar |
| 1 medium onion, cut in half | ¼ cup molasses |
| 1 teaspoon salt | Boiling water |

Rinse and pick over beans, removing any imperfect ones.

Friday night, put beans in a large bowl, cover with cold water, and soak overnight.

Drain beans and cover with fresh water in a large heavy saucepan.

Bring water just to a boil.

Preheat oven to 275°.

Place half the salt pork and the onion in the bottom of a 2-quart bean pot.

Drain beans and add to the pot.

Thoroughly mix salt, dry mustard, brown sugar, and molasses in 1 cup of boiling water. Pour mixture over beans.

Score remaining half of salt pork and place on top of beans.

Pour boiling water over all to the top of the bean pot.

Bake for 6–8 hours. Add a little more water during baking only if beans become dry.

# Broccoli Head with Lemon Butter

| | |
|---|---|
| 1 large head of Broccoli (1½–2 pounds) | Chicken broth (see Basic Chicken Broth recipe, page 89) |
| 1 teaspoon salt | |

Thoroughly wash and trim broccoli and cut off stem ends. Make diagonal cuts in stalk from stem up to flowerets.

---

\* Overnight recipe

Add broccoli head to 1 inch of boiling, salted chicken broth in a large, heavy saucepan.

Cover saucepan and cook broccoli rapidly for 10–12 minutes, or until just tender.

Drain immediately and place broccoli head in an atrractive pre-heated serving dish.

Drizzle hot lemon butter over broccoli before serving.

## LEMON BUTTER

**8 tablespoons (1 stick) butter**

**1 small lemon (juice)**

**2–3 sprigs fresh parsley, finely chopped**

Melt butter in a small saucepan over low heat.

Remove saucepan from heat and let butter stand for a few minutes until the solids settle at the bottom.

Skim butter fat from the top, and strain the liquid into another small saucepan or skillet.

Heat clarified butter very slowly over low heat until it turns a golden brown.

Stir in juice from the lemon and parsley.

Optional: ¼ cup toasted bread crumbs sprinkled over all.

## Broccoli Salad Appetizer

**2 large ripe tomatoes, coarsely chopped**

**2 large cloves of garlic, minced**

**1 small green pepper, minced**

**2 green onions (scallions) with tops, cut in 1-inch pieces**

**⅓ cup of olive oil**

**1 tablespoon wine vinegar**

**1 teaspoon salt**

**Generous sprinkling of freshly ground black pepper**

**1 large head of cooked broccoli, flowerets separated and stalks cut in 1-inch pieces**

Put tomatoes, garlic, green pepper, and green onions in a glass or pottery salad bowl.

In another small bowl thoroughly mix olive oil, vinegar, salt, and pepper.

Pour oil-and-vinegar mixture over vegetables and let stand for 2–3 hours, stirring occasionally.

Add broccoli and toss salad lightly but well before serving.

## Home-Fried Brussels Sprouts

1¼–1½ pounds (about 4 cups) cooked, fresh Brussels sprouts

1 egg, well beaten

¾ cup dry, fine bread crumbs

2 cups corn oil

Salt to taste

¼ cup grated Parmesan

Dip each Brussels sprout into egg and then roll in bread crumbs.

Heat 2 cups corn oil in a large heavy skillet. A piece of bread dropped into the oil will turn golden brown when the temperature of the oil is just right.

Fry sprouts quickly until brown, turning with a slotted spoon, about 1–2 minutes.

Remove sprouts from skillet with a slotted spoon and dry on absorbent paper.

Salt to taste.

Sprinkle grated Parmesan over all and serve immediately.

Note: Good as an unusual side dish with fried chicken.

## Brussels Sprouts Garden Special

2–3 green onions (scallions) with tops, cut in 1-inch pieces

1 small stalk celery, minced

1 small green pepper, minced

1 small carrot, minced

2–3 sprigs fresh parsley, coarsely chopped

4 tablespoons (½ stick) butter

1¼–1½ pounds (about 4 cups) cooked, fresh Brussels sprouts

Salt to taste

Generous sprinkling of freshly ground black pepper

In a large heavy skillet sauté green onions, celery, green pepper, carrot, and parsley in butter until tender-crisp.

Add Brussels sprouts and toss lightly until thoroughly mixed with vegetables.

Season to taste with salt and freshly ground black pepper.

Serve immediately right from the skillet.

## Watermen's Cabbage

1 large apple, cored, peeled, and coarsely chopped

1 medium onion, coarsely chopped

2 tablespoons bacon fat

1 medium-large head of cabbage, coarsely chopped

½ cup beer (or water)

½ cup dark brown sugar

½ cup cider vinegar

Salt to taste

Freshly ground black pepper to taste

In a large, heavy skillet sauté apple and onion in bacon fat for 10 minutes.

Into the apple and onion mixture, alternately stir in cabbage and beer (or water) a little at a time.

Continue cooking for 10–12 minutes, until cabbage is tender.

Thoroughly mix in brown sugar and vinegar.

Season with salt and freshly ground black pepper before serving.

## Church Creek Cabbage with Tart Sauce

4 tablespoons (½ stick) butter

1 teaspoon salt

1 teaspoon sugar

1 small lemon (juice)

1 tablespoon horseradish

½ teaspoon paprika

½ teaspoon fresh parsley, minced

Dash Tabasco sauce (optional)

1 medium-large head of cabbage, cooked and cut in quarters

Melt butter in a small saucepan and thoroughly mix in all other ingredients except cabbage.

Stir until sauce is hot but not boiling.

Arrange quarters of cabbage on a warm serving dish.

Pour sauce over all and serve immediately.

## Sunday's Country Slaw

*(6 servings)*

1 cup mayonnaise (see recipe, page 99)

2 teaspoons cider vinegar

½ teaspoon salt

¼ teaspoon white pepper

¼ teaspoon sugar

1 small head of cabbage, coarsely chopped

1 small onion, minced

1 small stalk celery, minced

1 teaspoon fresh parsley, minced

1 small carrot, cut in very thin strips

1 small green pepper, cut in very thin strips

Mix mayonnaise, vinegar, salt, pepper, and sugar in a small bowl.

Arrange cabbage, onion, celery, parsley, carrot, and green pepper in a salad bowl.

Pour dressing over all.

Cover salad bowl and refrigerate for 1 hour.

Toss slaw lightly but well before serving.

## Creamy Mashed Carrots

1–1½ pounds of carrots, scraped, trimmed, and cooked

1 small onion, minced

2 tablespoons (¼ stick) butter, melted

2 tablespoons warm heavy cream

1 teaspoon fresh parsley, minced

Salt to taste

Sprinkling of freshly ground black pepper

Mash carrots in a medium-size, heavy saucepan.

Add onion, melted butter, warm cream, and parsley.

Place saucepan over boiling water or very low heat and whisk carrots until smooth and creamy.

Season with salt and freshly ground black pepper and serve immediately.

## Jack's Carrot Burgers

| | |
|---|---|
| 1 cup of grated raw carrots | Dash of Worcestershire sauce |
| 1 small onion, grated | 2 tablespoons (¼ stick) butter |
| 2 cups of dry fine bread crumbs | 1 tablespoon bacon fat (or 3 tablespoons butter) |
| ½ teaspoon baking powder | Salt to taste |
| 1 egg, well beaten | Sprinkling of freshly ground black pepper |
| 2 tablespoons half-and-half (or milk) | |

Thoroughly mix carrots, onion, bread crumbs, baking powder, egg, and half-and-half (or milk), and Worcestershire sauce in a medium-size bowl.

Form carrot mixture into 8 small patties.

Wrap patties in waxed paper and refrigerate for 1 hour.

Heat butter and bacon fat (or just butter) in a medium-size, heavy skillet until just sizzling.

Brown carrot patties quickly on each side for 2–3 minutes.

Season with salt and freshly ground black pepper and serve immediately.

## Cauliflower Head with Egg Sauce

| | |
|---|---|
| 1 large head of cauliflower | Cold water to cover |
| 1 teaspoon salt | |

Clean and trim cauliflower head and let stand in cold salted water, head down, for 30 minutes.

Rinse cauliflower head in clear water and place in a large, heavy saucepan.

Add 1 teaspoon of salt and enough cold water to cover the head.

Bring water to a boil and cook cauliflower for 20–30 minutes until tender.

Drain and place head in an attractive preheated serving dish.

Pour Egg Sauce over the cauliflower before serving.


## EGG SAUCE

2 tablespoons (¼ stick) sweet (unsalted) butter

2 tablespoons all-purpose flour

½ teaspoon salt

1 cup half-and-half (or light cream)

2 hard-cooked eggs, finely chopped

2–3 sprigs fresh parsley, minced

1 small lemon (juice)

Melt butter in the top of a double boiler.

Stir in flour and salt with a wooden spoon and keep mixture warm over hot but not boiling water.

Slowly blend in half-and-half (or cream) and continue stirring until sauce is creamy and smooth.

Add chopped eggs, parsley, and lemon.

Blend well before pouring over cauliflower head.


# Countrifried Cauliflower

Cooked flowerets from 1 large head of cauliflower (discarding core and stems)

Salt to taste

Sprinkling of freshly ground black pepper

Sprinkling of paprika

2 tablespoons (¼ stick) butter

6 tablespoons (¾ stick) butter

¾ cup dry bread crumbs

1 teaspoon fresh parsley, minced

Sprinkle cauliflowerets with salt, freshly ground black pepper, and paprika.

Heat 2 tablespoons of butter in a large heavy skillet until just sizzling.

Add cauliflowerets and brown quickly for 2–3 minutes, turning with tongs or a slotted spoon.

Remove cauliflowerets from the skillet with a slotted spoon and set aside.

Heat 6 tablespoons of butter in the same skillet until just sizzling.

Add bread crumbs and brown well.

Return cauliflowerets to the skillet and toss lightly but well with the bread crumbs.

Sprinkle with parsley and serve immediately.

## Wye Mills Celery Casserole

*(6 servings)*

| | |
|---|---|
| **1 large bunch celery** | **2 large onions, thinly sliced** |
| **4 tablespoons (½ stick) butter** | **Salt to taste** |
| **1 tablespoon cornstarch** | **Generous sprinkling of** |
| **Water** | **freshly ground black pepper** |
| **2 cups chicken broth (see Basic Chicken Broth recipe, page 89)** | |

Preheat oven to 325°.

Thoroughly wash and trim celery and discard leaves. Cut stalks into 1-inch pieces.

Heat butter in a large, heavy skillet until just sizzling.

Add celery and brown quickly for 2–3 minutes.

Mix cornstarch with just a little water to form a smooth blend.

Combine cornstarch with 2 cups of chicken broth and pour over celery.

Reduce heat and continue cooking for 5 minutes.

Place onion rings in a shallow baking dish.

Pour celery and chicken broth over onions.

Bake for 1 hour, season with salt and pepper, and serve immediately.

## Southern-Fried Corn*

4 cups of cooked fresh corn
  kernels

½ teaspoon salt

Generous sprinkling of
  freshly ground black pepper

1 small onion, minced

1 small green pepper, minced

4 tablespoons bacon fat

Combine corn, salt, freshly ground black pepper, onion, and green pepper in a bowl.

Heat bacon fat in a large heavy skillet until just sizzling.

Place corn mixture in the skillet and reduce heat.

Cook corn over medium heat for approximately 20 minutes, stirring occasionally.

Use a spatula to scrape brown crust from the bottom of the skillet, and mix the crust in with the corn.

Serve immediately.

## Country-Style Creamed Corn

8 ears of corn

1 tablespoon butter

1 cup half-and-half (or light
  cream)

1 teaspoon salt

Generous sprinkling of
  freshly ground black pepper

1 teaspoon sugar

2 tablespoons (¼ stick) butter

Preheat oven to 350°.

Husk corn and remove silk. Cut kernels from the cob with a sharp knife, being careful not to cut too deep into the cob. Scrape juice and any remains of the kernels from the cob into a bowl.

Lightly grease an ovenproof casserole with 1 tablespoon butter.

---

* Good recipe for leftovers

Combine corn with juice and scrapings, half-and-half (or light cream), salt, pepper, and sugar in the casserole.

Dot with 2 tablespoons of butter.

Bake corn for 45–50 minutes, until kernels are tender.

## Hoopers Island Fried Cucumbers

*(6 servings)*

| | |
|---|---|
| **4 medium cucumbers** | **¾ cup dry bread crumbs** |
| **1 teaspoon salt** | **1 egg, beaten** |
| **½ teaspoon white pepper** | **¼ cup corn oil** |

Pare cucumbers and slice into ⅓-inch pieces.

Pat slices dry with paper towels.

Sprinkle cucumber slices with salt and white pepper.

Dip slices into bread crumbs, then into egg, and again into bread crumbs.

Heat corn oil in a large heavy skillet until just sizzling.

Brown cucumber slices quickly on each side for 1–2 minutes.

Drain slices on absorbent paper and serve immediately.

## Dossie's Elegant Picnic Eggplant

*(6 servings)*

| | |
|---|---|
| **1 medium-large onion, coarsely chopped** | **1 large ripe tomato, coarsely chopped** |
| **2 cloves garlic, minced** | **1 small carrot, thinly sliced** |
| **⅓ cup olive oil** | **2–3 sprigs fresh parsley, finely chopped** |
| **1 large green pepper, cut in thin strips** | **1½ pounds eggplant, peeled and diced** |
| **1 medium zucchini, cut in ½-inch slices** | **1 teaspoon olive oil** |
| **1 medium summer squash (yellow straight-neck), cut in ½-inch slices** | **Salt to taste** |
| | **Freshly ground black pepper to taste** |

In a large heavy skillet sauté onion and garlic in olive oil until golden.

Add green pepper, zucchini, summer squash, tomato, carrot, parsley, and eggplant.

Sprinkle olive oil over all.

Cover skillet and simmer vegetables over low heat for 45 minutes.

Uncover skillet and continue cooking for approximately 15 minutes, until most of the liquid is absorbed.

Season with salt and pepper.

Eggplant may be served warm or chilled.

Note: If serving chilled, drizzle a favorite oil-and-vinegar dressing over the eggplant and toss lightly but well.

## Garden-Fresh Greens

*Young* greens are tender greens, and they should be bright in color and have no wilted or yellow leaves.

Carefully pick over greens to remove any blemishes, dry leaves, tough stems, roots, etc.

Greens must be washed *thoroughly* under cold running water, and rinsed several times until they're absolutely clean.

Cook:

**GREENS**

| | |
|---|---|
| **Beet Tops**<br>**Collards**<br>**Dandelions**<br>**Kale**<br>**Turnips** | 10–15 minutes in ½ an inch of boiling salted water |
| **Mustard**<br>**Spinach**<br>**Swiss Chard** | 5–10 minutes in ½ an inch of boiling salted water |

or

Steam greens in a collander over boiling salted water for 10–25 minutes (depending on the leaves) until tender.

or

In a large heavy pot cook ½ pound of salt pork in 1 quart of boiling water for 1 hour. Add greens, cover pot, and cook for 15–20 minutes, until greens are tender.

Season with butter and/or salt and/or freshly ground black pepper and/or a few drops of vinegar (a Maryland favorite.)

Three pounds of greens will serve four.

Note: If cooking greens in salted water, or steaming, save the "pot likker" (the liquid from the greens) as a stock for soups and gravies.

## Ottie's Okra

1 small onion, finely chopped

1 small green pepper, finely chopped

3 tablespoons bacon fat

1 pound okra, stems removed, and cut in ½-inch pieces

1 large tomato, peeled, and coarsely chopped

1 cup cooked, fresh corn kernels

Salt to taste

Freshly ground black pepper to taste

Sprinkling of paprika

In a large, heavy skillet sauté onion and green pepper in bacon fat until tender-crisp.

Add okra and continue cooking for 5 minutes.

Mix tomato into the skillet and simmer for 15 minutes until okra is tender.

Add corn and stir vegetables lightly but well.

Season with salt, freshly ground black pepper, and paprika before serving.

## Tilghman Hash-Brown Parsnips

2 eggs, well beaten

1–1½ pounds parsnips, scraped, cooked, and mashed

½ teaspoon salt

3 tablespoons butter, melted

¾ cup half-and-half (or milk)

3 tablespoons flour

1 tablespoon corn oil

Combine eggs and parsnips in a medium-size bowl and mix well.

Thoroughly blend in salt, melted butter, half-and-half (or milk), and flour.

Heat 1 tablespoon of oil in a medium-size heavy skillet until just sizzling.

Add parsnip mixture to skillet and cover.

Cook until a brown crust forms on the bottom of skillet.

Use a spatula to scrape crust from bottom of skillet and turn parsnips over to brown on the other side.

Serve immediately when parsnips are brown and crusty.

## Peas in Blankets

1 small head of lettuce, washed, cored, and leaves separated

2 pounds of peas, shelled

1 teaspoon salt

1 teaspoon sugar

½ teaspoon white pepper

2 green onions (scallions) with tops, cut in 1-inch pieces

3 tablespoons butter

1 tablespoon cold water

Place several layers of lettuce leaves on the bottom of a large, heavy saucepan (with a tight-fitting lid).

Arrange peas on top of lettuce.

Season with salt, sugar, and white pepper.

Add green onions, 3 tablespoons of butter, and 1 tablespoon of water.

Top peas and onions with more layers of lettuce leaves.

Cover saucepan and cook peas over low heat for 20 minutes.

Lettuce leaves may be coarsely chopped and mixed in with peas and liquid before serving.

*(6 servings)*

8 medium potatoes, cooked, peeled, sliced, and chilled

1 medium onion, finely chopped

1 medium stalk celery, thinly sliced

1 small cucumber, peeled, seeded, and coarsely chopped

1 tablespoon fresh parsley, minced

3 hard-cooked eggs, coarsely chopped

1 cup mayonnaise (see recipe, page 99)

2 teaspoon prepared yellow mustard

1 teaspoon salt

Sprinkling of white pepper

1 small green pepper, cut in thin strips

1 small carrot, cut in thin strips

4–5 radishes, thinly sliced

6 pimiento-stuffed olives, cut in half

3 large ripe pitted olives, thinly sliced

Paprika

Place chilled potato slices in a large salad bowl with onion, celery, cucumber, parsley, and chopped eggs.

Thoroughly blend mayonnaise, mustard, salt, and white pepper.

Mix well with potatoes and toss lightly.

Garnish with green pepper and carrot strips, radishes, olives, and a light sprinkling of paprika.

Cover and chill for 1 hour before serving.

# Tart-and-Sweet Skillet Potatoes

*(6 servings)*

8 medium potatoes, cooked, peeled, and diced

4 slices bacon

1 medium stalk celery, finely chopped

1 medium onion, finely chopped

1 medium green pepper, finely chopped

2–3 sprigs fresh parsley, minced

2 eggs, well beaten

¼ cup sugar (or to taste)

¼ teaspoon dry mustard

½ teaspoon salt

Generous sprinkling of freshly ground black pepper

Sprinkling of paprika

½ cup cider vinegar

½ cup cold water

3 hard-cooked eggs, coarsely chopped

2 sweet gherkins, minced

1 medium apple (ripe), peeled, cored, and coarsely chopped

Keep diced potatoes warm.

Fry bacon in a large heavy skillet until brown and crisp.

Remove bacon from skillet with a slotted spoon, dry on paper towels, crumble, and set aside.

Add celery, onion, green pepper, and parsley to the skillet and sauté in bacon fat for 1–2 minutes.

Beat eggs in a medium-size bowl with sugar, mustard, salt, pepper, paprika, vinegar, and water.

Pour egg mixture into skillet and cook, stirring constantly, for 6–8 minutes, until sauce begins to thicken.

Add potatoes, chopped eggs, pickles, and apple and toss lightly but well with the egg mixture.

Continue cooking over low heat for another minute or so.

Sprinkle potatoes with crumbled bacon and serve right from the skillet.

# Maple-Candied Sweet Potatoes

*(6 servings)*

6 medium sweet potatoes, cooked, peeled, and sliced

½ cup maple syrup

2 tablespoons (¼ stick) butter

1 teaspoon salt

1 cup apple cider

½ cup cold water

½ cup unsalted walnuts or pecans, coarsely chopped (optional)

Preheat oven to 300°.

Arrange sweet potato slices in a shallow baking dish.

In a small heavy saucepan bring maple syrup, butter, salt, cider, and water just to a boil.

Sprinkle coarsely chopped nuts over sweet potatoes (optional).

Pour maple syrup mixture over sweet potato slices.

Bake for 1 hour.

# Roasted Pumpkin Seeds Snack

2 cups fresh pumpkin seeds, washed, hulled, and dried

1½ tablespoons peanut oil

1 teaspoon salt

Sprinkling of freshly ground black pepper

Sprinkling of garlic powder

Sprinkling of paprika

Preheat oven to 300°.

In a small bowl toss pumpkin seeds in a mixture of peanut oil, salt, black pepper, garlic powder, and paprika.

Spread pumpkin seeds out on a cookie sheet and roast until dry and crispy, approximately 30 minutes.

Shake cookie sheet occasionally so that seeds will brown evenly.

# Baked, Stuffed Winter Squash

2 large acorn squash

2 tablespoons (¼ stick) butter, melted

½ teaspoon salt

Sprinkling of freshly ground black pepper

1 small onion, minced

1 tablespoon corn oil

¼ cup soft white bread crumbs

2 tablespoons cold water

1 egg, well beaten

Sprinkling of salt

Sprinkling of freshly ground black pepper

¼ cup dry, fine bread crumbs

2 tablespoons (¼ stick) butter

Preheat oven to 325°.

Thoroughly wash squash, cut in halves, remove seeds and fibers, and wipe dry with paper towels.

Drizzle melted butter over each squash half and sprinkle with salt and freshly ground black pepper.

Bake squash cut side down on a cookie sheet until tender, 1–1¼ hours.

Remove squash from oven and increase heat to 375°.

Scoop out insides of squash and mash in a small bowl, setting squash shells aside.

In a medium-size, heavy skillet sauté onion in 1 tablespoon oil until golden.

Soak soft white bread crumbs in cold water and drain.

Make a pulp of bread crumbs and add to onions in skillet.

Add mashed squash to onions and bread and cook over low heat, stirring occasionally, for approximately 15 minutes.

Thoroughly combine beaten egg, salt, and pepper with squash.

Fill squash shells with mixture from the skillet.

Sprinkle dry bread crumbs over each squash half and dot with pats of butter.

Bake for approximately 20 minutes, until squash is nicely browned.

## Summer Squash Casserole
## (Zucchini)

1 small onion, coarsely
  chopped

1 large clove garlic, minced

1 small green pepper, coarsely
  chopped

1 medium stalk celery, thinly
  sliced

3 tablespoons olive oil

2 pounds zucchini, scrubbed
  and cut in ½-inch slices

2 large tomatoes, peeled and
  coarsely chopped

1 teaspoon salt

Generous sprinkling of
  freshly ground black pepper

1 tablespoon fresh parsley,
  minced

2 tablespoons grated Parmesan
  (optional)

In a large, heavy skillet sauté onion, garlic, green pepper, and celery in oil until soft.

Add zucchini slices, tomatoes, salt, freshly ground black pepper, and parsley.

Cover skillet and cook over low heat until zucchini is tender, 18–20 minutes.

Toss zucchini and vegetables lightly but well before serving.

Serve zucchini in an attractive preheated casserole, and sprinkle with grated Parmesan (optional).

## Trappe Green Tomato Fry

4 large green tomatoes, cut in
  ½-inch slices

1 teaspoon salt

Generous sprinkling of
  freshly ground black pepper

¾ cup all-purpose flour

¼ cup peanut oil

Pat tomato slices dry with paper towels.

Mix salt and freshly ground black pepper with flour.

Coat tomato slices on both sides with flour.

Heat peanut oil in a large heavy skillet until just sizzling.

Reduce heat and fry tomato slices on each side until brown and crusty, 1–2 minutes.

Drain tomato slices on absorbent paper and serve immediately.

## Old-Fashioned Scalloped Tomatoes

*(6 servings)*

6 medium tomatoes, peeled and coarsely chopped

1 teaspoon salt

Generous sprinkling of freshly ground black pepper

2 teaspoons sugar

1 small onion, minced

1 tablespoon butter

1½ cups croutons

2 tablespoons (¼ stick) butter

Preheat oven to 400°.

Place tomatoes in a medium-size heavy saucepan (with a tight-fitting lid).

Cover saucepan and cook tomatoes over low heat, stirring occasionally, for 15 minutes.

Season tomatoes with salt, freshly ground black pepper, sugar, onion, and 1 tablespoon butter.

Line bottom of a shallow baking dish with ½ cup of croutons.

Pour tomatoes over croutons.

Sprinkle remaining croutons over tomatoes and dot with 2 tablespoons of butter.

Bake for approximately 20 minutes, until nicely browned.

## Mary Ellen's Buttery Mashed Turnips

2 yellow turnips (about 2½–3 pounds) pared, and cut in small pieces for quick cooking

3 tablespoons butter

1 tablespoon warm heavy cream

1 teaspoon salt

Generous sprinkling of freshly ground black pepper

Add turnip pieces to 1 inch of boiling water in a large, heavy saucepan.

Cover saucepan and cook turnip for 20–25 minutes, until tender.

Drain turnip and thoroughly mash with butter and cream.

Season mashed turnip with salt and freshly ground black pepper and serve immediately.

# VEGETABLE TIPS!

- Cook vegetables in chicken or beef broth, instead of water, for a different taste, and reserve liquid. Vegetable broth may be frozen in an ice cube tray and the cubes stored in a tightly closed plastic bag in the freezer for later use in soups and stews.

- All greens should be dry before storing to preserve their crispness. Wash and dry greens just before cooking.

- To prevent eyes from watering when peeling onions, hold 1 or 2 wooden match sticks (with the striking end out) between your teeth. Try it!

- For both color and flavor, add thoroughly washed pods to the water when cooking fresh peas. Pods will float on top of water when peas are cooked.

- Plunge a tomato into boiling water for a few seconds and then into cold water to peel off skin easily. Add a few grains of sugar to tomatoes when cooking to bring out their flavor.

- A few drops of fresh lemon juice dropped in the cooking water will whiten boiled potatoes.

# BREADS AND BISCUITS

**THE RECIPES:**

BREAKFAST MUFFINS
GRANDMA'S WINTER FRY BREAD
30-MINUTE SNACKING CHEESE BREAD
HUSH PUPPIES
MR. FEATHER'S SPOON BREAD
MARIE'S IRISH SODA BREAD
FOOLPROOF POPOVERS
SUNDAY BISCUITS
WATERMEN'S COFFEE-CAN BREAD
SKIPJACK BEATEN BISCUITS
PRINCESS ANNE CARROT BREAD
CUSTARD CORN BREAD
     plus
PLAIN OR HERBED HOMEMADE BUTTER

# Breakfast Muffins

*(8 muffins)*

**2 tablespoons butter**
**1 egg, well beaten**
**½ cup milk**
**1 cup sifted all-purpose flour**

**Pinch of salt**
**1 teaspoon baking powder**
**1 tablespoon butter, for muffin pan**

Preheat oven to 400°.

Melt butter in a small, heavy saucepan and blend in egg and milk.

Sift flour, salt, and baking powder into a medium-size bowl.

Stir egg and milk into flour mixture, mixing until smooth.

Spoon batter into a buttered 8-muffin pan.

Bake muffins for 20 minutes.

Remove from muffin pan and serve immediately.

# Grandma's Winter Fry Bread

*(16 pieces)*

**4 cups unsifted all-purpose flour**
**2 tablespoons baking powder**
**1 teaspoon salt**
**2 tablespoons shortening**
**1 cup milk**

**¾ cup water**
**Sprinkling flour**
**Corn oil (2 inches in skillet)**
**Salt to taste**

Thoroughly mix flour, baking powder, and salt in a large bowl.

Add shortening and blend into flour with your fingers (or use a pastry blender), mixing well.

Stir milk into flour mixture.

Add water, a little bit at a time, until dough is formed. If dough is too stiff, add a few more drops of water.

Sprinkle a board and your hands with flour.

Knead dough well on the board 7 or 8 times and form into a ball.

Break off 16 pieces of dough (about 1½ inches thick) and flatten into a pancake approximately 5 inches in diameter.

Heat 2 inches of corn oil in a large heavy skillet or Dutch oven. A piece of bread dropped into the oil will turn golden brown when the temperature of the oil is just right.

Fry dough until golden brown about 2 minutes on each side.

Remove fry bread from skillet with tongs and dry on absorbent paper.

Salt to taste before serving.

Note: Fry bread may also be dusted with confectioners' sugar, instead of salt, for the "sweet teeth."

## 30-Minute Snacking Cheese Bread

*(8 slices)*

1 medium onion, minced

1 small clove garlic, minced

4 tablespoons (½ stick) butter

¼ cup chili sauce

2 teaspoons celery seeds

1 loaf of unsliced white bread (1 pound)

8 medium-thin slices of cheese (Muenster, mozzarella, Swiss, etc.)

Preheat oven to 350°.

Sauté onion and garlic in butter in a small heavy skillet until golden.

Stir in chili sauce and celery seeds and mix well.

Cut bread in 8 equal slices almost through to bottom crust.

Using half the chili sauce mixture, spread it between each slice of bread.

Add cheese between each slice.

Cover a cookie sheet with foil and place bread on the foil.

Pour remaining half of chili sauce mixture over top of bread.

Bake for 1 hour.

Remove bread from oven and cool for a few minutes before serving warm.

# Hush Puppies

*(12 pieces)*

1 cup stone-ground white
    cornmeal

1 teaspoon baking powder

½ teaspoon salt

1 small onion, minced

1 egg

½ cup milk or half-and-half

4 cups corn oil

Combine cornmeal, baking powder, salt, and onion in a medium-size bowl.

Beat egg into milk (or half-and-half) and blend well with cornmeal mixture.

Heat corn oil in a large, heavy skillet or Dutch oven. A piece of bread dropped into the oil will turn golden brown when the temperature of the oil is just right.

Form batter into 2 oblong shapes about 4 inches long, 2 inches wide, and ¾ inch thick; or shape into 12 cones.

Fry until golden brown, about 2–3 minutes.

Remove hush puppies from skillet or Dutch oven with a slotted spoon and dry on absorbent paper.

Note: Oil may be strained, refrigerated in a tight covered container, and used again (for all recipes).


# Mr. Feather's Spoon Bread

*(4–6 spoonfuls)*

2 cups water

1 cup stone-ground yellow
    cornmeal

3 tablespoons butter

1 teaspoon salt

3 large eggs, well beaten

1 cup light cream, warm

1 tablespoon butter, for dish

Preheat oven to 375°.

Bring 2 cups water to a boil in a medium-size, heavy saucepan.

Slowly stir cornmeal into boiling water, until mixture is smooth and mushy.

Remove saucepan from heat.

Beat in butter and salt, and cool mixture until just warm.

Blend in eggs and cream, and whisk for 2 minutes until smooth.

Pour batter into an attractive, buttered, casserole dish.

Bake for 30–35 minutes, until golden brown and firm.

Remove from oven and serve, using a large spoon to spoon piping hot bread onto plates.

Pass the butter!

## Marie's Irish Soda Bread

*(7" round loaf)*

**2 cups unsifted all-purpose flour**

**1 tablespoon sugar**

**1 teaspoon baking powder**

**1 teaspoon baking soda**

**½ teaspoon salt**

**3 tablespoons butter, softened**

**1 cup seedless raisins**

**1 cup buttermilk**

**Sprinkling flour**

**1 teaspoon butter, for baking sheet**

**1 tablespoon butter, melted, for brushing**

Preheat oven to 375°.

Sift flour, sugar, baking powder, baking soda, and salt in a large bowl.

Cut softened butter into flour with a fork or pastry blender, until mixture has the consistency of fine crumbs.

Add raisins.

Thoroughly blend buttermilk into flour with a fork, mixing until moist.

Turn dough out on a lightly floured board and knead it gently for a minute or so until smooth.

Shape into a ball and place on a buttered cookie sheet.

Flatten dough into a circle approximately 1½ inches thick and 7 inches in diameter.

Cut dough in quarters (with a floured knife) halfway through to bottom of loaf.

Bake 30–40 minutes, until top of bread is golden brown and the loaf has a hollow sound when tapped.

Brush top of bread with melted butter before serving.

## Foolproof Popovers

*(1 dozen)*

| | |
|---|---|
| **1 cup sifted all-purpose flour** | **1 cup cold milk** |
| **½ teaspoon salt** | **1 tablespoon butter, for muffin pan** |
| **2 eggs, well beaten** | |

Sift flour and salt over beaten eggs in a medium-size bowl.

Add cold milk.

Beat flour mixture until smooth and not too thick, the consistency of heavy cream.

Pour batter into a buttered 12-muffin pan so that each muffin mold is ⅔ full.

Place muffin pan in cold oven and turn temperature to 450°.

Bake for 30 minutes, until popovers are golden brown and puffy.

Remove from muffin pan and serve immediately.

## Sunday Biscuits

*(2 dozen)*

| | |
|---|---|
| **1¾ cups sifted all-purpose flour** | **¾ cup milk** |
| **½ teaspoon salt** | **Sprinkling flour** |
| **3 teaspoons double-acting baking powder** | **2 tablespoons (¼ stick) butter, melted, for brushing** |
| **6 tablespoons (¾ stick) butter** | |

Preheat oven to 450°.

Sift flour, salt, and baking powder into a large bowl.

Cut butter into flour with a fork or pastry blender, until mixture is the consistency of fine crumbs.

Blend milk thoroughly and quickly into flour with a fork until sides of bowl are clean and dough is formed.

Turn dough out on a lightly floured board, and knead it gently and quickly for half a minute, until smooth.

Roll dough out to approximately a ½-inch thickness.

Flour a 1½" biscuit cutter and cut out 2 dozen pieces of dough, or form dough with your hands.

Brush the tops of dough with melted butter.

Place dough on a cookie sheet.

Bake for 12–15 minutes, until tops of biscuits are nicely browned.

Remove biscuits from oven and set aside to cool.

Serve while still warm (or hot, if you prefer).

## Watermen's Coffee-Can Bread

*(2 loaves)*

**4 cups unsifted all-purpose flour, separated**

**1 package active dry yeast**

**½ cup half-and-half, or milk**

**½ cup water**

**½ cup corn oil**

**¼ cup sugar**

**1 teaspoon salt**

**2 eggs, beaten**

**2 tablespoons butter, for coffee cans**

Preheat oven to 375°.

Combine 2 cups flour and yeast in a large bowl.

Heat half-and-half (or milk), water, corn oil, sugar, and salt in a small, heavy saucepan until just warm.

Pour liquid into bowl with flour and yeast.

Beat well, until batter is smooth.

Blend in eggs.

Add remaining 2 cups of flour gradually and continue beating well until batter is smooth and elastic. Add a little more flour if necessary.

Divide batter between 2 well-buttered 1-pound coffee cans with plastic snap-on lids.

Cover cans with lids and set aside in a warm place for dough to rise 1 hour.

When dough has risen almost to the top of cans, remove plastic lids.

Bake for 30–35 minutes until bread is puffed up and nicely browned.

Remove cans from oven and set aside to cool for approximately 15 minutes.

Turn bread out of can and set on rack to finish cooling.

## Skipjack Beaten Biscuits

*(2 dozen)*

**2 cups unsifted all-purpose flour**

**½ teaspoon salt**

**1 teaspoon shortening**

**1 cup cold water**

**Sprinkling flour**

Preheat oven to 325°.

Combine flour and salt in a medium-size bowl.

Cut shortening into flour with fingers or a fork.

Gradually add water to make a stiff dough.

Roll dough out on a board. (Now the fun starts, and this is an *easy* version of the famous Maryland Beaten Biscuits!)

Beat dough with a mallet or hammer to a ½-inch thickness.

Fold dough over in 5–6 layers and beat again.

Continue folding and beating dough 6 or 7 times, or for approximately 30 minutes, until it becomes smooth and elastic.

When finally beaten, roll dough out to a ½-inch thickness.

Flour a 1½" biscuit cutter and cut out 2 dozen pieces of dough, or form dough with your hands.

Prick the middle of each piece of dough with a fork, place dough on a cookie sheet and bake for approximately 30 minutes, until edges of biscuits are hard and tops are slightly browned.

Remove from oven and set aside to cool.

Biscuits may be stored in a tightly covered jar for a week.

## Princess Anne Carrot Bread

*(9 × 5 loaf)*

1½ cups sifted all-purpose
   flour

1½ teaspoons baking soda

1 teaspoon cinnamon

¾ cup sugar

2 eggs, well beaten

1 cup corn or peanut oil

1 teaspoon salt

1 teaspoon vanilla

1½ cups grated raw carrots

1 tablespoon butter, for loaf
   pan

Preheat oven to 350°.

Sift flour with baking soda and cinnamon in a medium-size bowl.

Add sugar, eggs, oil, salt, and vanilla.

Whisk grated carrots into mixture and blend well.

Pour batter into a buttered 9 × 5 loaf pan.

Bake for 1 hour.

Remove pan from oven and set aside to cool for approximately 15 minutes.

Turn loaf out of pan and set on rack to finish cooling.

## Custard Corn Bread

*(8" square)*

| | |
|---|---|
| ¼ cup sifted all-purpose flour | 9 ounces of milk |
| 1 tablespoon sugar | 1 egg, well beaten |
| ½ teaspoon salt | 2 tablespoons (¼ stick) butter |
| 1 teaspoon baking powder | ½ cup milk |
| ¾ cup stone-ground white cornmeal | |

Preheat oven to 400°.

Sift flour, sugar, salt, and baking powder into a large bowl.

Add cornmeal.

Blend in milk and egg, and whisk mixture briskly for approximately 1 minute.

In the oven melt butter until just sizzling in an 8 × 8 baking pan.

Pour batter into pan.

Pour the milk over the batter, and *do not stir*.

Bake for approximately 30 minutes, until set.

Serve hot, right from pan.

## Plain or Herbed Homemade Butter

*(about ¼ pound)*

| | |
|---|---|
| ½ pint heavy cream | Fresh herbs to taste (your choice of chives, dill, parsley, garlic, etc.) |
| Pinch of salt | |

Beat cream in a medium-size bowl until water separates from it. Use either an electric or a rotary beater (the rotary takes a few minutes more).

Pour off liquid and season the butter that remains with salt and your choice of herbs, to taste.

Spoon butter into an attractive serving dish, or smooth into a mold and unmold before serving.

# BREAD TIPS!

- To make bread crusty, dilute one of those leftover egg whites mentioned in this book with 1 tablespoon cold water. Brush on top of bread 5 minutes before baking is finished.

- Lightly oil the cup in which you measure molasses, honey, and other sticky ingredients.

- Knead dough with the heel of your hand (it's the coolest part of the hand).

- Put flour and water in a small jar with a tight-fitting lid and shake vigorously for instant and smooth thickening for a recipe.

- To make toasted bread cups, ready for filling, trim crusts and cut full rounds from fresh bread. Press bread rounds into a lightly buttered muffin pan and place in a 350° oven until golden brown.

- Use a *hot* knife to cut fresh bread easily.

# SWEETS

## THE RECIPES:

COTTAGE BREAD PUDDING

LAZY-DAY CARAMEL APPLES

STONE JAR GINGERSNAPS

OLD-FASHIONED VANILLA ICE CREAM

MOCHA CUSTARD

GREEN TOMATO BROWN BETTE

TRIPLE-FRUIT SHERBET

QUICK-'N-EASY PICNIC CUPCAKES
   WITH SUGAR ICING

JENNIE'S TOASTED NUT STRIPS

MISS NELLIE'S GINGERBREAD

FISHING CREEK BLUEBERRY DUMPLINGS

GRAPE FLUFF

NO-CRUST CHOCOLATE FUDGE PIE

CAP'N HARRINGTON'S GOOEY PEARS

CHEWY BUTTERSCOTCH BROWNIES

MAMA'S TOMATO SPICE CAKE
   WITH CREAM CHEESE FROSTING

# Cottage Bread Pudding

*(6 servings)*

2 cups white bread cubes

1 cup small-curd cottage cheese

1 cup milk

½ cup half-and-half

4 tablespoons (½ stick) butter, melted

2 eggs, well beaten

¼ cup sugar (⅓ cup for a sweeter pudding)

Sprinkling of salt

½ teaspoon allspice

¼ teaspoon mace

¼ teaspoon ground cloves

¼ cup seedless raisins

¼ cup walnuts, finely chopped

1 tablespoon butter, for dish

Preheat oven to 325°.

Thoroughly combine bread cubes, cottage cheese, milk, half-and-half, and melted butter in a medium-size bowl.

Blend in eggs, sugar, salt, allspice, mace, cloves, raisins, and walnuts, and mix well.

Pour bread mixture into a buttered baking dish.

Bake for 1 hour or until a knife inserted in the middle of pudding comes out clean.

Serve hot or cold with mounds of freshly whipped cream.

# Lazy-Day Caramel Apples

1 pound vanilla caramels, coarsely chopped

1 tablespoon butter

2 tablespoons cold water

6 wooden skewers

6 medium apples, red and crisp

½ cup walnuts, finely chopped

Melt caramels and butter with water in the top part of a double boiler.

Thoroughly stir caramels with a wooden spoon, over boiling water, until mixture is creamy and smooth.

Remove double boiler from heat.

Stick a wooden skewer in the stem end of each apple.

Dip each apple in caramel mixture until completely coated and then roll in chopped walnuts. (Add a few drops of water if caramel mixture begins to thicken, and stir well.)

Place apples on sheets of waxed paper and let stand until firm.

## *Stone Jar Gingersnaps*

*(about 9 dozen gingersnaps)*

1 cup shortening

1 cup sugar

⅔ cup hot, strong, black coffee

⅔ cup molasses

5 cups cake flour

½ teaspoon salt

1 teaspoon baking soda

1 teaspoon ground ginger

1 teaspoon ground cloves

½ teaspoon cinnamon

2 tablespoons (¼ stick) butter, for cookie sheets

Preheat oven to 350°.

Thoroughly cream shortening and sugar in a large bowl.

Blend hot coffee with molasses and stir into shortening and sugar.

In another large bowl sift cake flour with salt, baking soda, ginger, cloves, and cinnamon.

Add flour to coffee and molasses and mix well, forming a soft dough.

Wrap dough in waxed paper and refrigerate for 1 hour.

Roll dough out on a board to a thickness of approximately ⅛ inch.

Cut out dough with a round cookie cutter 2 inches in diameter.

Place dough on lightly buttered cookie sheets.

Bake for 5–8 minutes, until brown. Watch gingersnaps closely to prevent scorching (molasses burns quickly).

Remove cookies from oven and set aside to cool.

Note: Gingersnaps may be stored in a stone jar with a tight-fitting lid. Otherwise, store gingersnaps in a large cookie jar with a tight-fitting lid to keep them crisp for two weeks or more.


# Old-Fashioned Vanilla Ice Cream

*(about 1 quart)*

**3 egg yolks**
**1 cup milk**
**½ cup sugar**
**Sprinkling of salt (about
⅛ teaspoon)**

**1 tablespoon pure vanilla
extract**
**1 cup heavy cream, whipped**

Separate eggs, putting yolks in a small bowl and set whites aside for another use.

In the top part of a double boiler, away from heat, whisk egg yolks and milk until well blended.

Stir in sugar and salt.

Cook over hot but not boiling water, stirring constantly, until mixture is thick and creamy.

Remove from heat and pour custard mixture into a medium-size bowl.

Set aside to cool, and then cover and refrigerate until chilled.

Stir vanilla extract into the custard mixture.

Place custard mixture in your refrigerator's freezer for approximately 1 hour, until partially frozen and mushy.

Remove custard mixture from freezer and beat until smooth and creamy.

Fold in whipped cream and blend well.

Pour mixture into a freezer container large enough to leave approximately 1 inch at the top of the container.

Cover and freeze for 3 hours, until ice cream is firm, stirring the custard 2 or 3 times during the first hour of freezing.

## Mocha Custard

1 ounce unsweetened chocolate, finely chopped

1 cup hot, strong, black coffee

1 cup half-and-half

¼ cup sugar

1 tablespoon light brown sugar

2 eggs (unbeaten)

Sprinkling of salt

Preheat oven to 300°.

Combine chocolate, coffee, half-and-half, sugar, brown sugar, eggs, and salt in a medium-size bowl.

Beat until creamy and smooth. (A blender or electric beater may be used for a smoother custard.)

Pour mixture into an attractive baking dish or mold.

Set the baking dish/mold in a shallow pan of hot water (1 inch).

Bake for 1 hour until custard is firm and a knife inserted near the edge comes out clean.

Remove custard from the oven and set aside to cool.

Cover and refrigerate custard until ready to serve.

Note: Custard may be sprinkled with slivered almonds and milk chocolate before serving.

## Green Tomato Brown Bette

*(6 servings)*

5 medium green tomatoes, coarsely chopped, and drained

1 teaspoon cinnamon

¼ teaspoon ground cloves

¼ teaspoon nutmeg

1 teaspoon grated lemon peel

2 tablespoons (¼ stick) butter

1 cup dark brown sugar

2 cups dry, fine bread crumbs

6 tablespoons (¾ stick) butter, melted

1 tablespoon butter, for dish

1 lemon (juice), separated

Preheat oven to 350°.

In a large, heavy skillet simmer tomatoes, cinnamon, cloves, nutmeg, and lemon peel in 2 tablespoons of butter for 5 minutes.

Add brown sugar and stir over low heat for 10 minutes more.

Thoroughly blend bread crumbs with melted butter in a small bowl.

Press ⅓ of the bread crumbs into an attractive, buttered, shallow baking dish.

Spoon half the tomato mixture over bread crumbs.

Sprinkle with half the lemon juice.

Top tomato mixture with another third of the bread crumbs.

Layer remaining tomatoes on top of bread crumbs.

Sprinkle with remaining half of the lemon juice.

Top with rest of the bread crumbs.

Cover baking dish and bake Brown Bette for 40 minutes.

Raise oven temperature to 400°.

Remove cover and bake for 10 more minutes until nicely browned.

Remove Brown Bette from oven and set aside until warm.

Serve warm, topped with mounds of freshly whipped cream.

## Triple-Fruit Sherbet

*(6 servings)*

1 ripe banana, peeled and mashed

½ cup fresh orange juice

2 tablespoons fresh lemon juice

½ cup sugar (¾ cup for a sweeter sherbet)

Sprinkling of salt

1 cup evaporated milk, chilled

2 tablespoons fresh lemon juice

Thoroughly blend banana with orange juice, 2 tablespoons of lemon juice, sugar, and salt.

Pour mixture into a refrigerator freezing tray, and chill thoroughly.

In a small bowl, beat chilled milk until light and fluffy.

Add 2 tablespoons lemon juice and continue beating until milk is stiff.

Fold into fruit mixture and mix lightly.

Freeze without stirring until sherbet is firm.

## Quick-'n-Easy Picnic Cupcakes with Sugar Icing

*(12 cupcakes)*

| | |
|---|---|
| **1½ cups cake flour** | **½ cup vegetable shortening** |
| **½ teaspoon salt** | **1 teaspoon baking powder** |
| **1 cup sugar** | **½ teaspoon baking soda** |
| **½ cup milk** | **½ cup boiling water** |
| **1 egg** | **1 teaspoon pure vanilla extract** |
| **½ cup cocoa** | **12 paper cupcake cups** |

Preheat oven to 325°.

Sift cake flour and salt together in a large bowl.

Thoroughly blend in sugar, milk, egg, cocoa, shortening, baking powder, baking soda, boiling water, and vanilla.

Beat mixture well for approximately 3 minutes until well blended.

Place paper cups in a muffin pan.

Divide batter equally among the paper cups and bake for 30 minutes.

Remove cupcakes from oven and set aside.

## SUGAR ICING

| | |
|---|---|
| **2 cups confectioners' sugar** | **1 teaspoon pure vanilla extract** |
| **Sprinkling of salt** | **1 tablespoon heavy cream** |

Sift confectioners' sugar with salt into a small bowl.

Stir in vanilla extract.

Beat heavy cream into the sugar mixture to make a good spreading consistency for the cupcakes.

Coat each cupcake with icing and pack them up for the picnic!


## Jennie's Toasted Nut Strips

*(1 dozen)*

1 egg
¼ cup half-and-half
½ teaspoon salt
1 teaspoon sugar
4 slices white bread (1 inch thick), crusts removed, and cut in 1-inch strips

1 cup peanuts, almonds, walnuts, or pecans, finely chopped
1 tablespoon butter, for cookie sheet

Preheat oven to 450°.

Thoroughly beat egg, half-and-half, salt, and sugar in a small, shallow dish.

Dip bread strips in egg mixture and then roll in chopped nuts.

Place bread strips on a buttered cookie sheet.

Bake for 15 minutes.

Remove from oven and set aside to cool.


## Miss Nellie's Gingerbread

*(6 servings)*

3 cups all-purpose sifted flour
1 teaspoon cinnamon
1 teaspoon ground ginger
1 teaspoon ground cloves
1 teaspoon baking soda
1 cup dark brown sugar

½ cup shortening, melted
1 cup molasses
2 eggs (unbeaten)
1 cup boiling water
1 tablespoon butter, for pan

Preheat oven to 350°.

Sift flour, cinnamon, ginger, cloves, and baking soda in a large bowl.

In a separate small bowl stir brown sugar into melted shortening.

Add molasses and eggs and beat well.

Blend brown sugar mixture slowly into flour, alternating with small amounts of boiling water and beating thoroughly after each addition.

Pour mixture into a buttered 10 × 10 baking pan.

Bake for 25 minutes.

Serve hot with vanilla ice cream or mounds of freshly whipped cream.

## *Fishing Creek Blueberry Dumplings*

*(6 servings)*

**3 cups fresh blueberries**        **2 teaspoons baking powder**

**⅔ cup sugar**                     **¼ teaspoon salt**

**1 cup cold water**                 **½ cup light cream**

**1 cup all-purpose flour**

Simmer blueberries, sugar, and water in a large, heavy saucepan over low heat.

Combine flour, baking powder, and salt in a small bowl.

Thoroughly blend in cream and mix well.

Bring blueberries to a boil in saucepan and cook for 1 minute.

Drop 6 spoonfuls of batter in separate mounds on top of blueberries.

Reduce heat, and cover saucepan with a tight-fitting lid.

Cook blueberries over low heat for 20 minutes, until dumplings are puffy and a toothpick inserted in them comes out clean.

Serve blueberries and dumplings in small soup bowls or ramekins.

# Grape Fluff

*(6 servings)*

1 tablespoon unflavored
    gelatin

1½ cups grape juice, separated

¼ cup sugar

¼ teaspoon salt

1 tablespoon fresh lemon juice

2 egg whites

¼ cup heavy cream, whipped

Soften gelatin in ½ cup grape juice for 5 minutes.

Heat remaining cup of grape juice, sugar, salt, and gelatin in a medium-size, heavy saucepan.

Stir over low heat until dissolved.

Add 1 tablespoon lemon juice.

Remove grape mixture from heat and set aside to cool and thicken.

Separate eggs, putting whites in a small bowl and setting yolks aside for another use.

Whisk egg whites briskly until stiff and peaks form.

Fold egg whites gently, but well, into grape mixture.

Fill six parfait glasses with ⅔ of the mixture.

Add whipped cream to remaining grape mixture and fill the glasses.

Chill until firm before serving.


# No-Crust Chocolate Fudge Pie

*(8″ pie)*

2 ounces unsweetened
    chocolate, melted

1 cup sugar

8 tablespoons (1 stick) butter,
    softened

2 egg yolks

⅓ cup flour

1 teaspoon pure vanilla extract

1 cup walnuts, pecans, or
    almonds, coarsely chopped

2 egg whites

Pinch of salt

1 tablespoon butter, for pie
    plate

Preheat oven to 325°.

Melt chocolate in a small heavy saucepan and set aside to cool slightly.

Thoroughly cream sugar and butter in a large bowl.

Separate eggs, putting yolks in a small bowl and setting whites aside for later use.

Beat yolks and cooled chocolate into sugar and butter.

Blend in flour, vanilla, and nuts and beat well.

Whisk egg whites and pinch of salt in a small bowl until stiff and peaks form.

Fold egg whites gently, but well, into chocolate batter.

Pour batter into a buttered 8″ pie plate.

Bake for 30 minutes.

Serve fudge pie topped with vanilla ice cream or mounds of freshly whipped cream.

## Cap'n Harrington's Gooey Pears

*(8 servings)*

**4 large, ripe pears, peeled, cored, and cut in half**

**½ lemon (juice only)**

**8 heaping teaspoons dark brown sugar (or light, if you prefer)**

**1 cup heavy cream, warm**

Preheat oven to 400°.

Rub pear halves with lemon juice.

Arrange pears in a shallow baking dish large enough to hold the halves comfortably together.

Place 1 heaping teaspoon brown sugar in each pear half.

Bake pears for 20–25 minutes, until sugar becomes caramelized.

Pour warm cream in the bottom of the baking dish.

Turn off oven and let pears sit for 20 minutes.

Remove pears from oven and set aside.

Spoon sauce over warm pears and serve immediately.


## Chewy Butterscotch Brownies

*(3 dozen)*

**8 tablespoons (1 stick) unsalted butter**

**2 cups light brown sugar**

**2 eggs**

**1½ cups all-purpose flour**

**2 teaspoons baking powder**

**1 teaspoon pure vanilla extract**

**1 cup walnuts or pecans, finely chopped**

**1 tablespoon butter, for pan**

Preheat oven to 350°.

Melt butter in a large heavy saucepan over low heat.

Thoroughly blend in brown sugar and bring to a boil.

Stir well with a wooden spoon and remove saucepan from heat.

Set saucepan aside and cool mixture for 5–8 minutes, but do not let mixture harden.

Add eggs one at a time to sugar and butter, and beat the mixture well after each addition.

Sift flour with baking powder and thoroughly blend into saucepan.

Stir in vanilla extract and chopped nuts.

Mix well, and pour mixture into a buttered 13 × 9 baking pan.

Bake for 30 minutes.

Remove from oven and let cool.

Cut into 36 squares.

Note: Brownies may be stored in an air-tight container for a few days (*if* you have any left to store!).

# Mama's Tomato Spice Cake with Cream Cheese Frosting

*(6–8 servings)*

¾ cup shortening

1¼ cups sugar

2 eggs

1 can condensed tomato soup

¾ cup cold water

1 teaspoon baking soda

3 cups sifted all-purpose flour

1 tablespoon baking powder

1 teaspoon cinnamon

½ teaspoon nutmeg

½ teaspoon of pumpkin pie spice, or ground cloves

½ cup walnuts

Preheat oven to 350°.

Thoroughly cream shortening and sugar in a large bowl.

Add eggs and beat well.

Mix soup, water, and baking soda.

Sift flour, baking powder, cinnamon, nutmeg, pumpkin pie spice (or cloves) in a large bowl.

Add flour mixture slowly to shortening and sugar, alternating with small amounts of tomato soup, and beating thoroughly after each addition.

Stir in walnuts.

Pour batter into a bundt pan and bake for 55 minutes.

Remove cake from oven and set aside to cool for 1 hour.

Turn cake out on a rack and cover with cream cheese frosting.

## CREAM CHEESE FROSTING

1½ cups confectioners' sugar

3 ounces cream cheese

1 teaspoon pure vanilla extract

Thoroughly blend sugar, cream cheese, and vanilla in a small bowl.

Beat well until light and fluffy.

Frost cake and serve.

# SWEET TIPS!

- To soften brown sugar that has become hardened, place a crisp lettuce leaf or a slice of fresh bread in the container.

- Lightly dust cakes or cupcakes with flour so that icing won't run off sides.

- Before adding raisins to any recipe, plump them in boiling water for 4–5 minutes.

- Butter or margarine wrappers, kept in your refrigerator, are ideal for greasing baking pans.

- Use confectioners' sugar instead of flour when rolling out cookies or other pastry dough. Cookies and other dessert recipes will be only slightly and not noticeably sweeter.

- Always let a cake cool before icing (unless otherwise specified).

- Cut an apple in half and put it in the container with your cakes to keep them fresh.

- A pinch of salt added to heavy cream will make it whip better and faster. A pinch of salt will also bring out the flavor of any recipe that contains chocolate.

- Soak whole nuts in their shells overnight in salt water before cracking. Nutmeat will come out whole and firm.

# QUICK CHECKLIST
# FOR WEIGHTS
# AND MEASURES

**Liquid:**

1 tablespoon = 3 teaspoons
2 tablespoons = 1 ounce
4 tablespoons = ¼ cup
5 tablespoons + 1 teaspoon = ⅓ cup
8 ounces = 1 cup
2 cups = 1 pint
4 cups = 1 quart
2 pints = 1 quart
4 quarts = 1 gallon
1 cup heavy cream = 2 cups whipped cream

**Dry:**

16 ounces = 1 pound
8 quarts = 1 peck
4 pecks = 1 bushel
1 stick butter = 8 tablespoons = ½ cup = ¼ pound
2½ cups white sugar = 1 pound
2½ cups brown sugar = 1 pound
3½ cups confectioners' sugar = 1 pound
1 pound all-purpose flour = 4 cups sifted flour
1 cup raw rice = 3 cups cooked rice

# INDEX

Triple-Fruit Sherbert, 158–59
Turnip
  -Apple Relish, 105
  Buttery Mashed, Mary Ellen's, 138–
    39
Turnip Greens, Garden-Fresh, 130–31

Vanilla Ice Cream, Old-Fashioned, 156
Vegetable(s)
  Chicken and, Tossed in a Skillet, 64–
    65
  -Chicken Chowder, Farmers', 93
  Soup, Old-Fashioned Crock, 86
  tips on, 139
  *See also* Specific Vegetables

Velvet Cream Sauce for Chicken, 106–7

Watercress-Cucumber Soup, Smedley's
    Landing, 83
Watermen's Cabbage, 123
Watermen's Coffee-Can Bread, 147–48
Watermen's Fish Chowder, 89–90
Watermen's Oyster Pie, 37–38
Winter Cabbage Soup, 94
Winter Squash, Baked, Stuffed, 136
Wye Mills Celery Casserole, 127–28

Zucchini Casserole, 137